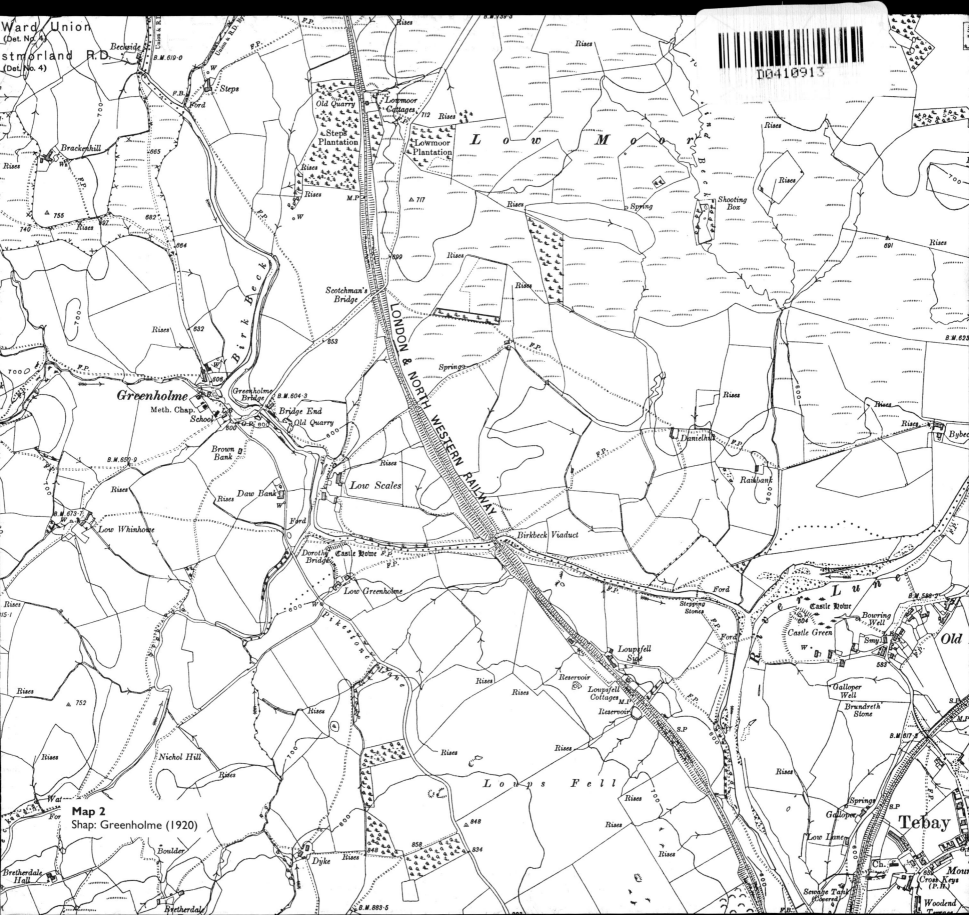

Map 2
Shap: Greenholme (1920)

Ivo Peters'
FAREWELL TO
NORTH-WEST STEAM

Ivo Peters' FAREWELL TO NORTH-WEST STEAM

Edited by Mac Hawkins

*A photographer's salute
to the last days of steam
over Shap and on the Settle & Carlisle*

DAVID & CHARLES

Front cover
Dillicar troughs
91 NY 612025
Westmorland at its best: the splendour of the countryside is evident in this shot of two Stanier Class 5 4–6–0s, headed by No 44672, as they pass over Dillicar troughs on their run north with a down parcels train. The train engine is 'taking a dip', whilst the fireman of No 44672 leans out of the cab to check the goings-on, his engine obviously having enough in reserve. Sheep graze undisturbed in the meadow between the line and the meandering course of the River Lune, visible on the left of the picture. *14 April 1966.*

Back cover
Cowperthwaite
97 SD 610964
Stanier Class 5 No 45045 heads a special southbound freight and approaches Cowperthwaite as it rounds the bend from Lowgill. In the background are the beautiful Howgill Fells. *14 April 1966.*

Greenholme
91 NY 602059
Nearing Scotchman's Bridge at Greenholme ex-LMS Class 5 No 45449 plods uphill with a northbound goods, assisted in the rear by Fairburn 2–6–4T No 42210. *13 April 1966.*

Frontispiece
91 NY 612025
Ivo Peters took this photograph at the same moment as Angela O'Shea, of two Stanier Class 5s, No 44672 acting as pilot, with a northbound parcels train passing over Dillicar troughs in the Lune Gorge; her colour version appears on the front jacket. *14 April 1966.*

A DAVID & CHARLES BOOK
Colour photographs and text copyright © Mac Hawkins, 1992
Black and white photographs copyright © Julian Peters
First published 1992

A catalogue record for this book is available from the British Library.

ISBN 0 7153 0080 6

Book designed by Michael Head
Typeset by Ace Filmsetting Ltd, Frome
and printed in Great Britain by Butler & Tanner
for David & Charles
Brunel House Newton Abbot Devon

CONTENTS

Note: All photographs are accompanied by grid references denoting the points from where they were taken. The references given are derived from the Ordnance Survey 1:50,000 series of Landranger maps and are accurate to 50 metres.

Map 3
Shap: The Lune Gorge (1920)

INTRODUCTION

Mention the Fells or the Dales and most railway enthusiasts will immediately conjure up in their minds romantic images of the rugged but magnificent Cumbrian countryside through which two important railways were constructed in the last century. Both the former LNWR route (West Coast main line) to Scotland and the Midland Railway's Settle–Carlisle route were brilliantly engineered, with many impressive structures like the Batty Moss Viaduct at Ribblehead on the latter. This area of the North-West provided the ideal landscape to see steam locomotives working at their hardest in a hostile although scenic environment as they tackled the long and steep gradients that challenged them on either route, particularly the arduous climbs to Blea Moor on the Settle & Carlisle and to Shap Summit on the West Coast main line— and often in atrocious weather conditions.

The majestic leviathans of the steam age seemed to blend in naturally with the remote grandeur of the Fell and Dale countryside, which provided a superb backdrop for the skilled railway photographer to capture them on film for posterity. Now much of this countryside has changed forever, for the passage of the M6 threads its way through the Fells, some would liken to a giant snake entwining its victim in a deadly embrace; nevertheless it is equally well engineered as the railway and has won recognition for its sympathetic construction through an outstand-ingly beautiful area. Where the railways once ruled supreme and went unchallenged, they are now almost overshadowed by modern man's folly in succumbing to his unremitting love of the motor vehicle, which has necessitated the building of a modern motorway network and other road improvements. Many of the scenic and tranquil settings, particu-larly the Lune Gorge, the photographers of twenty-five years ago enjoyed can never be recaptured; its serenity has been irrevocably scarred, mainly by the incessant noise of traffic. Even the railway running through it has sprouted masts along its course carrying the wires of the 25kV electrification system of the West Coast main line completed in 1974, some six years after the demise of steam. In reality this is little worse than the multitude of telegraph poles and wires that once adorned the lineside, which sometimes made photography difficult to say the least!

Ivo Peters, whose name has become synonymous with the Somerset & Dorset railway, was without doubt one of the finest and most skilled photographers ever to have visited this region—albeit in the last three years of the steam era, when diesels were already hauling most of the express passenger traffic. It was only after much persuasion from his friend and fellow photographer, the late Derek Cross, that Ivo was prised away from his beloved Somerset & Dorset line, which by 1964 was already in its death throes. In April 1965 he made the first of several trips to Westmorland and to the Yorkshire Pennines to record the dying days of steam on the West Coast main line and Settle–Carlisle route. By then the few remaining steam locomotive classes, predominantly Stanier 'Black Fives', were mainly confined to that part of the country and were generally in an appalling external condition. Few of the previously named classes like the Britannia Pacifics still carried their nameplates, usually having been unofficially removed as souvenirs; and often even the locomotives' numbers would be totally obscured by layers of grime and filth.

This then was the swansong of steam and a far cry from the halcyon days of just a few years before, when these giants went unchallenged and one still could occasionally see a gleaming LMS Coronation Pacific at the head of an express, which reflected the pride some shedmasters took in turning out a much-loved charge. The last scheduled run by this class over Shap was a London–Glasgow express relief working on 1 September 1964, when No 46254 *City of Stoke-on-Trent*, a 5A Crewe (North) locomotive, performed the honour. All remaining Coronations, with the exception of No 46256 *Sir William A. Stanier, F.R.S.*, which continued to run specials into the October, were withdrawn before the end of the month. With the demise of these mighty Pacifics and the race to modernisation, it was only the last glowing embers of a once-glorious age that were recorded by Ivo. His final visit to the North-West was

91 NY 608007
The Lune Gorge today: this view taken on 3 April 1992 looking south-east shows the proximity of the M6 to the West Coast main line. Ivo Peters' perch on the bluff on Dillicar common used to be on the far bend, ahead of the southbound freight train, where it has been carved through by the motorway. *(Author)*

made in August 1967, literally weeks or days before many of his subjects were consigned for scrap and only four months prior to the last steam working over Shap—which was on 31 December—and exactly a year before BR steam finally passed into the annals of history.

Usually staying for a week at a time in the Shap Wells Hotel, which became his 'headquarters' and from where he conducted his photographic forays, Ivo visited many of the most picturesque railway locations in the area to record both still and moving pictures of steam hauled trains passing through the region's dramatic countryside. He did not confine his photography solely to steam engines, but also occasionally recorded their diesel usurpers, which he dubbed 'stinkers'! Often on these visits, as indeed he was on the first, Ivo was accompanied by his great friend Norman Lockett, also a keen railway photographer and to whose memory he wished this book to be dedicated. Travelling from his home in Bath, occasionally Ivo would also invite his long-time housekeeper, Mrs Angela O'Shea, to accompany them on these safaris. An accomplished photographer in her own right, she had specialised in taking photographs of churches—her first love. However, Ivo encouraged her to record on colour film the dying days of steam, particularly on the Somerset & Dorset; but as a result of the trips north, her collection includes many taken in Westmorland, which complement the superb black-and-white photographs and the 16mm movie film taken by Ivo, much of which is now available on video. Some of the subjects featured in this volume are also replicated on film. With his skill as a photographer and by the excellent printing of his negatives, a first rate collection of photographs was assembled some twenty years ago for publication in a book to be called *Happiness Remembered*, a title which reflected the pleasure he obtained from these trips. Because of Ivo's other publishing commitments, mainly in producing the splendid books on the Somerset & Dorset, which ran to several volumes and proved to be best sellers, this particular book was never completed and remained untouched for several years.

In the early 1980s Ivo Peters became seriously ill, eventually bedridden and no longer able to pursue his skills as a photographer. It was shortly before he died in June 1989 that he suggested the book be resurrected under the title of *Farewell, Westmorland Steam*. Having written the introductory text, and knowing he was not well enough to be able to complete the work, he asked the writer if he would undertake the task in order that it could be finished; but with other work already commissioned, regrettably this was unable to be done before Ivo died in the summer of that year.

Three years after his death the book has been resurrected using Ivo's original title to head the text he wrote as an illustrated introduction to its main photographic theme.

It was at Ivo's particular request, and as a personal tribute to her, that a selection of Angela O'Shea's excellent colour slides taken during these visits—often simultaneously with his black-and-white shots—should be featured. In addition, with the kind permission of his son Julian Peters, the book also includes a selection of photographs Ivo took on the Settle & Carlisle line during this period, most of which have never been published before. A change of title was therefore necessary: a small price to pay for the Settle & Carlisle's inclusion, especially since this dramatic and much-loved railway route was recently under threat of closure, but reprieved at the eleventh hour. Ivo Peters would surely have approved of this change of heart. This book is a valuable record of these visits to the North-West, as his superb photographs will testify.

Mac Hawkins COSSINGTON, 1992

Note: The following text was written by the late Ivo Peters as a background and an introduction to this book, which he wished to be dedicated to his great friend Norman Lockett, and remains largely unaltered, as he would have wished. Since it was his original intention for this volume to concentrate solely on the West Coast main line through Westmorland, now Cumbria, no mention was made in this passage of his few visits to the Settle & Carlisle line, which he equally enjoyed, therefore its inclusion as a separate section in this volume is an added bonus.

HAPPINESS REMEMBERED

by Ivo Peters

DEDICATION

To the memory of the late Norman Lockett
—an outstanding railway photographer
and delightful friend and companion on so many of
my photographic expeditions.

Grayrigg, Lowgill, the Lune Gorge; Tebay, Greenholme, Shap Fell; even now just the mention of names like these is enough to stir my heart a little as so many happy memories come flooding back, only to be followed by a feeling of sadness at the realisation that it is all over, for never again will traceries of steam regularly thread the valleys and climb the fells of this most beautiful part of England. Although I photographed trains for over fifty years nowhere did I derive so much pleasure from this as in Westmorland—now known as Cumbria. The massive remote grandeur of the Fell country completely captivated me. For me, this was the ideal setting in which to film and photograph that majestic, lovable beast, the steam locomotive, which seemed to blend in so naturally with these wonderful surroundings.

On looking back, I often think of how very nearly I did not get up to Westmorland in time. That I did eventually do so was due entirely to my friend the late Derek Cross, the well-known railway photographer. For years Derek had been trying to persuade me to visit Shap but, loath to leave my beloved Somerset & Dorset line, I had produced one excuse after another for not making the long journey north from Bath. Then, in the late summer of 1964, whilst Derek was staying with me for one of his photographic sessions on the Somerset & Dorset, he succeeded at last in convincing me of what I was missing by not visiting Shap. So early in 1965 I wrote to the London Midland Region applying for a photographic permit covering the line from Oxenholme to Penrith, a privilege which they most kindly granted me, and in April I found myself at last motoring north towards Westmorland.

With me on this first expedition, and also to be my companion on many of the subsequent visits, was my friend the late Norman Lockett. We had first met back in 1956. I remember the occasion well—it was about six o'clock on the evening of 30 May and I had gone to Bath Spa station to photograph the 5.00pm down local from Swindon which was often used as a running-in turn for locomotives after they had been through the Works. As I walked towards the end of the up platform I noticed another photographer already in my position, a large amiable looking gentleman of about my own age, busily making adjustments to a vast and most impressive Quarter Plate Press camera. As, with a feeling of some inferiority, I took my elderly Agiflex camera out of its case, I mentioned—by way of breaking the ice—that I had photographed the train the previous evening in dull conditions at Saltford when the locomotive had been one of the 47XX class 2–8–0s *(Plate i)*. My companion, who turned out to be Norman Lockett, replied that he also had seen the 2–8–0 and was hoping that she would be on again this evening. However, in the event, it was a King class 4–6–0 that came into view round the bend—No 6009 *King Charles II*, just ex-works and in immaculate condition, her fresh paintwork gleaming in the early evening sunshine *(Plate ii)*.

But I am digressing—we were on our way up to Westmorland. I never looked forward very much to this 240-mile journey. Motorway driving, particularly after the introduction of the 70mph speed limit, I found monotonous—and then there was that awful forty minutes spent in negotiating the outskirts of Birmingham and Wolverhampton between the end of the M5 and the start of the M6. However, once we had crossed the high bridge over the Manchester Ship Canal I used to feel that the back of the journey was broken and my spirits would begin to rise, in anticipation of the pleasures that lay ahead. Both of us would start studying the sky to the north in an endeavour to assess the weather prospects, although there was an unwritten agreement between us that neither of us ever said that it looked as if the sun was going to shine. Many years back, we had found that this remark invariably produced rain—rather like when a commentator at a cricket match says a batsman is playing particularly well, he is often out the very next ball.

Normally, our visits to Westmorland were for a week at a time. We would leave Bath at eight o'clock in the morning so as to be in the vicinity of Grayrigg by about half past one. Between approximately a quarter to one and a quarter to two in the afternoon there used to be

i
Looking resplendent, having just undergone a works overhaul at Swindon, Churchward mixed-traffic Class 47XX 2–8–0 No 4708 sets off from Saltford, between Bath and Bristol on the GW main line, on an evening running-in turn with the 5.00pm Swindon–Bristol local train. The locomotive was painted in unlined black. No 4708 was withdrawn in October 1962. *29 May 1956.*

iii *(right)*
97 SD 606962
An unexpected appearance: on a very hot, hazy day in August, one of the few remaining ex-Crosti boilered 9F 2–10–0s, No 92021, with a southbound freight cautiously approaches Grayrigg, where it is about to be tucked away into the up loop to allow the passage of an express. *7 August 1967.*

ii
With its immaculate paintwork gleaming in the early sunshine, No 6009 *King Charles II* approaches Bath Spa station with the 5.00pm Swindon–Bristol local. The engine had just completed a works overhaul at Swindon, which included the fitting of a twin blastpipe and double chimney; it was to spend almost another sixteen years in service before withdrawal from traffic in September 1962. It was on this occasion Ivo Peters first met Norman Lockett, who was similarly engaged in photographing the train. Soon they were to become firm friends, and a few years later were to travel to Westmorland together. *30 May 1956.*

a procession of up expresses—unfortunately by 1965 all diesel hauled—and our aim was to be in position at our pre-selected spot in good time for the flurry of freights which so often followed in the wake of these expresses.

I remember on one occasion we had decided to spend our first afternoon in the Lune Gorge. It had been an excellent run up from Bath and we were running some twenty minutes ahead of our normal schedule as we made for Lowgill where we were going to leave the car. Descending the lane leading to the bridge over the line at the east end of Grayrigg, Norman Lockett, who understood timetables far better than I did, commented that the last of the up expresses was not due for another fifteen minutes, and jokingly, I said he had better put on his blinkers as we did not want to be lured away from our prearranged plans by anything that he might see at Grayrigg. However, as we were driving slowly over the bridge there suddenly came the eager cry from my passenger: "Something is signalled coming south and is being put into the loop!" Prearranged plans would have to wait, I hastily parked the car on the grass verge and we de-bussed at speed. Almost certainly this was a freight about to be tucked away out of the road of the express. A quick scramble over the wall and we were in position just in time as a clinking of buffers from round the bend to our north heralded the cautious approach of a freight. As the train came into sight neither of us at first could identify the strange locomotive at the head, but as she drew nearer we quickly realised with delight that it was one of the few remaining ex-Crosti 9F 2–10–0s—and the sun was shining (*Plate iii*). The opportunity of a second bite at this cherry was just too good to miss, so, getting back into the car, we drove round the lanes leading to the small overbridge at the west end of where Grayrigg station used to be, arriving just as a Brush Type 4 diesel swept through with the express. After a few minutes, there came the metallic thump as the points were changed and the ex-Crosti got the road to ease her train gently out of the loop and resume her journey southwards in the wake of the express. Once more the sun was shining as we got our second bite at this interesting cherry (*Plate iv*).

I shall never forget the first time I discovered this location at the west end of Grayrigg. It was about six o'clock one evening towards the end of April 1965; a storm was brewing and the fells to the east stood out dramatically against a background of menacing black thunder clouds. In the near distance, the fresh green larch trees in the small wood behind Grayrigg signal box were picked out by low shafts of sunlight and the whole area round me was bathed in golden evening sunshine. I found the scene really magnificent; all that was needed to complete the picture was a southbound steam-hauled train. If only one would come, I

thought, before the sun was swallowed up by the rapidly increasing storm clouds; but it was not to be—no train came south. However, just before the sun was finally obliterated, a northbound diesel-hauled express thundered through and I filmed the fast receding coaches as they swept away out of sight into the cutting beyond the Grayrigg box. Whenever I look at this piece of film I think of how marvellous it must be to be a great artist like David Shepherd or Terence Cuneo and to be able to reproduce on canvas the magnificence of such a scene. If I had been blessed with such talent I think I would roll back the years to about 1924: the northbound diesel-hauled express would become a southbound train in LNWR 'plum and spilt milk' livery hauled by a Claughton just repainted in LMS red.

After this first dramatic experience of what the west end of Grayrigg had to offer, I went back time and again over the next three years, always hoping for the chance to photograph a southbound steam-hauled train under similar conditions. Evening after evening we would end our day's photography at Grayrigg, arriving at the small bridge over the line at the western end at about a quarter to six; there was no point in getting there any earlier as the sun was not round far enough until at least five thirty (*Plate v*). Then, in April 1967, almost two years to the day since my original visit, came the evening for which I had always hoped. Once again a storm was building up to the east and there were the same dramatic lighting conditions. No sooner had we arrived than the signals came off for a southbound train. No express was due so surely it must be a freight—was this at last to be the opportunity for which I had longed? With mounting excitement I heard the train coming—only to have my hopes dashed as from out of the cutting came a diesel coasting leisurely along with empty stock (*Plate vi*). Ten minutes later, and with the lighting even more dramatic than when the diesel had come by, the signals came off again for another southbound train, and, once again, no express was due. There was hardly a breath of wind as we listened anxiously to catch the first trace of sound of the approaching train—then both of us heard it at the same moment, the distant, unmistakable, deep growling of a diesel travelling at speed; but this was coming from behind us—a northbound express was coming up the bank from Oxenholme. She had not got the road yet, but even as we noticed this,

iv
97 SD 597960
". . . a second bite at this interesting cherry". Photographed from the small overbridge (No 89) to the west of the former station at Grayrigg, the ex-Crosti 9F leaves the up loop to continue its journey with its mixed freight train. The shed code disc has already been removed from the smokebox door, but No 92021 was from Birkenhead (8H) MPD. *7 August 1967*.

v
97 SD 597960
The time is 5.40pm: even with the sun not yet far enough round for the
photographer's liking, a superb view looking east from the small overbridge at the
west end of Grayrigg is still to be had of Stanier 'Black Five' 4–6–0 No 45105 as it
passes by with a southbound freight. The 12A shed code signifies the locomotive
as one from Carlisle Kingmoor MPD. *14 July 1966.*

vi
97 SD 597960
"Was this at last to be the opportunity for which I had longed?" Dramatic lighting conditions are experienced as a thunderstorm builds up over the Howgill Fells in the distance, which provide a superb backdrop to Grayrigg in the foreground, bathed in evening sunlight. Ivo Peters' quest to capture a steam-hauled freight in these conditions was to be thwarted when this 1,250hp Birmingham Railway Carriage & Wagon Company-built Type 2 diesel-electric No D5355 (Class 27 TOPS No 27009) loomed into view with a southbound empty stock train. This class of locomotive was rarely seen south of Carlisle on the line over Shap. No 27009 was withdrawn in July 1980. *21 April 1967.*

vii
90 NY 557201
Ample smoke from the chimney of Stanier Class 5 4–6–0 No 45039 fortuitously blots out distracting electricity pylons and telegraph poles as it passes under the minor road bridge at Thrimby Grange and forges south with an up fitted freight. *13 April 1966.*

the down home signal rose lazily into the 'off' position. With the sound of the diesel getting steadily nearer we kept our eyes glued on the cutting where the southbound train would come into sight—the sun was still out and looked like remaining so for the next five minutes by which time, surely, our train would have come by. Then suddenly, there she was, a gleaming 9F 2–10–0 in charge of a fitted freight coming slowly into view from out of the cutting—oh, for heaven's sake, why would not she hurry? From the deep reverberating sound of the diesel, the northbound express was almost upon us. The two trains passed each other precisely where it made it quite impossible to get any picture. As their sound died away, the sun went in and my misery was complete. Although I kept on visiting this spot at Grayrigg until the end of steam I no longer felt I would get the picture that I wanted so much—and I never did.

In contrast to the disappointment at Grayrigg, I had considerable good fortune at another location near Thrimby Grange. I had found a spot which appealed to me greatly, where the line, running parallel to a small stream, passed underneath an attractive stone bridge. There was, however, a snag—in the background were several large electricity pylons and some tall telegraph poles. The only hope of a picture would be if the exhaust from the locomotive was sufficiently dense and also hung in the air long enough to obscure these background eyesores. A cold spring day with little or no wind seemed to offer the best chance of obtaining these conditions—and one afternoon in early April 1966 I got precisely what I wanted. Not one, but three freights came up the bank, one after the other, all producing the right exhaust conditions and all in sunshine *(Plate vii)*.

Norman Lockett had not been with me on my first visit to this spot near Thrimby Grange, so when we were up together in the following July we went along one afternoon in order that he could try his luck at this location. Leaving my car in the lane that led down to the bridge, we got over the wall into the field and walked down to the stream. Unlike my first visit, it was a hot afternoon and the only hope of having the pylons and poles obscured would be by dense smoke. We were about one hundred yards upstream from the bridge and settled ourselves comfortably in the shade of a convenient may tree to await developments. After a while I thought I heard the last of the southbound procession of diesel-hauled expresses coming up the bank, but then realised that the sound was coming from a large lorry descending the lane towards our bridge. To my surprise—for it was a very minor road—two more lorries then appeared in the wake of the first and I watched a little anxiously as all three slowly squeezed past where I had left my car. A little further on they pulled up, one behind the other, and next,

several men appeared on the bridge, looking first this way and then that. Eventually they spotted us basking under our tree and started waving. What a friendly gesture, we thought and waved back, but this did not seem to satisfy them. After a pause, one of the men—who we learned later was the foreman—negotiated with difficulty the wall and came across the field towards us. Suddenly, the awful thought struck me that perhaps the lane had not really been quite wide enough after all and one of the lorries had grazed the side of my car, but happily it was not this. With a friendly "Good afternoon" the man asked if it was our car in the lane. Yes, I said. Well, he replied, could I please move it as they wanted to do some tarring and gritting. More heavy diesel sounds now heralded the approach of a vast, yellow painted road roller, so with my car's well-being in mind, I thought perhaps the sooner I complied with his request the better. Whilst I was moving my car, the southbound express had passed and as I returned across the field to rejoin Norman, we caught the first sounds of a hard-working steam locomotive coming up the bank towards us. It was a Britannia class Pacific on an express freight and throwing out masses of black smoke to obscure half the countryside as well as the offending pylons and telegraph poles. Hastily adjusting the cine camera on the tripod, I filmed this exciting spectacle, but the events of the previous ten minutes must have been too much for me for I failed to notice that I had no film in the camera.

Whilst on the southbound climb up to Shap Summit, another spot comes to mind which used to hold out interesting photographic possibilities—Hardendale, some three and a half miles south of Thrimby Grange. There was a large quarry here and most mornings a locomotive could be found engaged on what was known as the 'Hardendale shunt'. On some days during shunting operations, the engine would reverse back to a point where the line curved round towards BR and here she would stand on her own for ten minutes or so. In the background was the main line—about one hundred yards away—and *if* the locomotive stopped in the right place and *if* a steam-hauled train happened to pass by on the main line during those ten minutes, then one got a rather interesting and unusual picture *(Plate viii)*.

When visiting a new locality for the first time it was always a bit of a gamble choosing the hotel at which to stay. Sometimes one was

viii
90 NY 570133
The 'Hardendale shunt': an interesting picture of Class 9F No 92112 standing at the entrance to the quarry as 'Black Five' No 44677 passes by on the main line with a down mixed traffic stock train. The driver of the 9F waves to his colleagues on the 4–6–0, but draws no response, whilst his fireman squatting on a rail is plainly intent on enjoying a leisurely cup of tea with the guard and takes no notice of the passing train. *22 September 1966.*

16

lucky—as Norman Lockett and I were on our first visit to the Isle of Man, when we picked an absolute winner—but on our initial Westmorland expedition we did not exactly hit the nail on the head the first time. The small hotel at which we stayed was homely and most reasonable in its charges, but we soon discovered one major snag—the evening meal had to be taken by seven thirty at the latest. Now in the late afternoon or early evening there often used to be a procession of northbound freights and it seemed a shame to have to miss the chance of seeing these on their climb from Tebay up to Shap Summit. Equally well, at the mature age Norman and I had reached, neither of us exactly relished the idea of going without our evening meal.

So on our next visit we decided to try another hotel and I picked on the Shap Wells Hotel which, apart from serving dinner up to nine o'clock in the evening, had the added attraction of being only about a quarter of a mile from the line *(Plate ix)*. This new choice turned out to be an ideal one in every way. The management and staff were most friendly and co-operative and soon got used to some of our more odd ways such as going out at six o'clock in the morning to photograph trains and then coming back to the hotel some three hours later for a quick breakfast before dashing out again. After a day or so the head waiter had things organised to a T. On arriving back at the hotel we would find our breakfast—and our picnic lunches—ready waiting for us and in next

ix
91 NY 578096
The Shap Wells Hotel, where Ivo Peters stayed during his trips to Westmorland, proved an ideal base from which to mount his photographic expeditions.

to no time, so it seemed, we would be setting off again for the line. For me, it was all rather reminiscent of a quick pit stop in my pre-war motor racing days.

After our first visit we always used to ask for the same rooms which were located in a recently converted stable block situated at the back of the hotel on the opposite side of a courtyard to the main buildings. These rooms were very comfortable and quiet, which suited me down to the ground, for I never enjoyed the noise and bustle of a large hotel. I remember one night waking up at about 2.00am and looking out of my bedroom window. The Fells, for as far as the eye could see, were bathed in the soft, silver light from a full moon and the only sound to break the stillness of the night was the quiet murmur of the Birk Beck which passed close below my bedroom window. Then, very faintly at first, I caught the distant beat of a steam-hauled freight climbing up from Tebay. Lying in bed listening to the sound getting gradually closer, I tried to identify from the beat the type of locomotive on the train, but fell asleep again almost at once. Far better than counting sheep!

The main entrance to the Shap Wells Hotel is down a long drive from the A6, but I always used a back way in off the Orton–Shap road. In 1965 this was really little more than a narrow track which curved down the side of the fell before passing underneath the railway and then heading straight across an open field to reach the hotel about a quarter of a mile further on *(Plate x)*. The stretch from the road down to the railway was only wide enough for one car, and in addition was bounded by a ditch on either side, so making it virtually impossible for two cars to pass. Whenever we approached this section Norman Lockett would jocularly inquire if I had the single line token, and I would invariably reply in the affirmative. But on one occasion as we were making a cautious approach to pass under the line, a cow suddenly shot out from beneath the railway heading straight for us. From the speed at which she was travelling it was quite obvious that our bovine friend was under the firm impression that she held the token and not us, so I stopped in a hurry. No sooner had she squeezed past us at a rollicking gait than a second cow appeared from out of the archway in pursuit of the first. At least, I thought it was a second cow but Norman then pointed out that it was different from the first one and was, in fact, a bull! He passed us at an even greater speed and by the sound he was making was definitely on full regulator and maximum cut-off. With some trepidation we then resumed our journey and on passing underneath the railway and emerging into the field we were amused to see several cows all gazing anxiously towards the archway and obviously wondering what had happened to Bessie!

About a quarter of a mile further up the bank from this archway under

x
91 NY 581098
The narrow back road to the Shap
Wells Hotel was gained from the
Orton–Shap road and passed under
the line at this point. This picture of a
heavy goods climbing Shap shows
Stanier Class 5 4–6–0 No 45449
passing over the archway (Bridge 116)
at the head of a fifty-wagon train,
which was banked by Fairburn 2–6–4T
No 42210. *13 July 1966.*

the line was the spot from which many of the best known photographs of Shap have been taken, including those superb pictures by the late Bishop Eric Treacy. For this reason we christened the location 'Classic'. On a fine day 'Classic' was a wonderful spot from which to watch trains climbing Shap; one could follow their progress for the whole of the five miles as they toiled up the bank from Tebay in the valley far below. I recall in particular one glorious evening in August 1967: it had been one of those days during which the weather got steadily better and better until by late afternoon conditions were near perfect with tremendous visibility. From our vantage point at 'Classic' the view was absolutely magnificent—the rising ground behind the line was one mass of purple heather whilst in the far distance the Fells stood out a soft blue grey against great towering banks of cumulus. In these glorious conditions we then had an almost continuous procession of freights up the bank *(Plate xi)*. No sooner had one come blasting up past us than a cloud of smoke and steam suddenly rising above the small hill hiding Tebay would herald the start of another banked freight setting off on the long climb up to the summit.

On hot summer evenings we would stroll out to 'Classic' again after dinner as dusk was gathering. I never ceased to be thrilled by the sight of a heavy freight storming up the bank towards me in the gathering darkness, the staccato beat of the exhaust growing in intensity as the train drew nearer and nearer. Great volumes of smoke, studded with showers of sparks, would be shooting high in the air from the locomotive's chimney and the exhaust, streaming back over the cab, would glint a lurid red as it was caught in the fierce glow from the open firebox doors. As the locomotive forged past in a crescendo of effort one caught a glimpse of the silhouetted figure of the driver sitting impassively at his controls, staring straight ahead, and the fireman, brilliantly lit by the harsh glare from the fire, toiling away with the shovel. As the pounding beat of the leading locomotive started to fade one became aware of the rising, more insistent note of the banker's exhaust as her shadowy outline at the tail of the train drew nearer. Then, with much hissing and clanking, she would be past and as the sound of the cavalcade gradually died away in the distance the stillness of the night would return to the fell.

I have always tended to wake up early in the morning, a habit which stood me in good stead on my visits to Westmorland for many of my best film sequences were shot before seven o'clock in the morning. As soon as I woke up, usually round about five o'clock, I would get out

of bed and walk over to the open window to survey the weather prospects. More often than not the outlook was pretty bleak—if it was not actually raining, then the whole sky would be a sullen, unbroken grey. But, just occasionally, the scene would be dramatically different and at the sheer beauty that met my eyes would murmur an involuntary "God Almighty" not irreverently, but in wonder and acknowledgement of the magnificence that confronted me. Surely dawn on a clear, still morning when the sky is streaked with colours of infinite softness and beauty must be one of Nature's masterpieces.

On mornings when the weather was at all reasonable we would lose no time in getting up and going out to the line. So as not to disturb the other residents in the hotel we would tiptoe out to the car parked in

xi
91 NY 580100
This was the location dubbed 'Classic' by Ivo Peters and surely testifies that the name was aptly accorded. Here 'Black Five' No 44858 is photographed climbing Shap with a northbound parcels train. This location had been a favourite haunt of many photographers for generations past as they too witnessed the struggle of steam engines tackling the arduous four-mile section at 1:75 between Tebay and the summit, often in typically appalling weather conditions. On a clear day, such as this, the spectacular views to the fells in the distance added to the rugged beauty of the location. *11 August 1967.*

xii
91 NY 595079
About to be stopped by the signals at Scout Green, Britannia Pacific No 70028 (ex-*Royal Star*) approaches from the south with a down freight. Banking in the rear is one of the ubiquitous 2–6–4Ts from Tebay shed (12E), which were the most common form of assistance afforded to freight trains on their climb to Shap Summit. *Royal Star* was one of a second batch of Britannias built and numbered among five (70025–29) originally allocated to Cardiff (Canton) shed, where the crews, unlike other WR men suspicious of anything 'non-Swindon', quickly became used to their quirks, and, by contrast, earned a satisfactory reputation with them. *22 April 1967.*

the courtyard and set off as quietly as possible. We often had a laugh at the thought that any resident who did happen to observe one of these departures of ours would obviously have suspected that we were doing an early morning flit without paying the bill!

A location which appealed to me greatly for filming on Shap in the early morning was the approach to Scout Green. It was possible to stand well back up the fell on the east side of the line and get a long pan as freights laboured up to Scout Green box. For 'still' photography this vantage point had a snag—not only were the telephone wires on the east side of the line but the poles also carried a thick black cable which was attached about half way up each pole. Between six and eight o'clock in the morning there was often a procession of northbound freights up the bank one after the other at regular intervals. However, I remember one morning at Scout Green when things were not quite so 'regular'. We had already been treated to two northbound freights, both banked, when a third appeared, unbanked, and obviously making very heavy weather of the climb. The locomotive was a 'Black Five' with steam oozing from all sorts of places where it should not have done, and as she laboured up past us her speed was down to a little better than walking pace. Long after she had passed out of sight behind a bluff in the hill a great cloud of slow moving black smoke continued to indicate her painfully slow progress towards Shap Wells. Then something made me look south. Two towering columns of exhaust were moving fast through the cutting at Greenholme—another banked freight was coming up and almost certainly would have to be stopped at Scout Green. Into view she came, a long freight headed by a Britannia and banked by a 2–6–4T (Plate xii). The home signal was on but the Britannia's driver made no whistle protest as he closed his regulator—doubtless like us he had ample visual evidence that the section ahead was still occupied by the ailing 'Black Five' and her train. A few minutes later, however, the preceding freight must have at last reached the summit, for the Britannia got the road and, in an effort to get her long train on the move again, proceeded to give a Vesuvian demonstration of some magnitude (Plate xiii). Eventually, with much slipping by the Pacific and steady, solid pushing by the 2–6–4T, the cavalcade was on the move again.

There was more than an element of luck connected with the best film sequence I ever got at Scout Green. It was just after sunrise on a bitterly cold morning in early April 1965. As we dropped down the narrow road leading towards the level crossing at Scout Green box we saw that the signal was off for something coming up the bank. Obviously there was no time to be lost. Hurriedly I swung the car off the road onto a convenient piece of flat ground and grabbed the cine camera and tripod. After the warmth of the car the cold hit me with a bang—the ground underfoot was frozen solid and everything was covered in a white frost. As I slipped and slithered my way up the side of the fell I could see from the exhaust that the train was already past Greenholme and less than a mile away. My fingers numb with cold I fumbled to erect the tripod and mount the camera. There was no time for the usual practice pans, for the train was almost within range—a quick adjustment of the aperture and I started filming. Up she came steadily towards us, a heavy freight hauled by a 'Black Five' and banked by a 2–6–4T. Both locomotives were working hard and leaving a glorious exhaust trail which hung almost motionless in the cold still air and stretched back

out of sight round the bend almost half a mile away. It had been touch and go, but I had got my shot although at the end of the pan I fear the train looks as if it is going down hill rather than up hill due to the tripod setting having been slightly out.

When I showed my friends the results of my 1965 filming on Shap, and this Scout Green sequence came up, I said proudly that it had been taken at six thirty in the morning. This brought forth ribald laughter and disbelief, so on my next visit to Shap I sought means of establishing visual evidence of the time of my early morning activities. It struck me that the church clock at Orton, a village only two miles from the line at Scout Green, would do very well. So one morning round about six thirty I drove into the small lane leading to Orton church and started to get the cine camera lined up on the church clock. Suddenly I got the feeling that I was being watched and then realised, somewhat to my embarrassment, that several pairs of eyes were gazing curiously at me from behind the lace curtained windows of cottages in the lane. Well, I suppose there is something a little odd about a complete stranger wanting to film your church tower at half past six in the morning.

Greenholme was another favourite spot of mine and we would often pay two visits here in the same day, starting off with a session in the early morning and then coming back again in the afternoon (Plate xiv). The reason for these split visits was that we were always optimists and based all our arrangements on the assumption that the sun would shine. When this did actually happen, lighting conditions for photography from the east side were excellent up to about ten o'clock, whilst from early afternoon onwards the sun would be far enough round for us to operate from the west side. For 'still' photography I found Greenholme, in some ways, a better early morning location than Scout Green, for where the line entered the cutting the telegraph poles had been moved further away from the track and it was possible to take up a position so that the thick black cable, although still a nuisance, did not offend quite so much. However, as Greenholme was only about a mile up the bank, any train that did not stop at Tebay for a banker would still be

xiii
91 NY 595079
". . . a Vesuvian demonstration of some magnitude"; Britannia No 70028, struggling to gain adhesion, makes rather an effort to restart—even with rear end assistance—as it sets off towards Scout Green signal box, a few yards north of this point and up the 1:75 rising gradient towards Shap Summit. The fireman has obviously done his work well, for he appears to be casually reading his newspaper and takes no notice of the exertions of his charge, which has steam to spare. Note the box's down home signal on the extreme right of the picture. *Royal Star* had not long to live, being withdrawn the following September, as were all the remaining Britannias by the end of the year. *22 April 1967.*

xiv
91 NY 602059
Another favourite spot on the climb to Shap. Seen from the west side of the line with its ample exhaust drifting in a typically stiff westerly wind, Stanier Class 5 No 45093 climbs from Tebay and approaches Greenholme with a heavy oil train with banking assistance from a 2–6–4T. *15 April 1965.*

xv
91 NY 602058
". . . on days when the rain never stopped": an unidentified Stanier Class 5 plods up past Greenholme in the rain with a heavy freight train, assisted in the rear by a 2–6–4T; the gloomy conditions belied the fact that it was high summer! Shap Summit lay some four miles distant. *13 July 1966.*

moving pretty fast as it came by, and more than one driver who had decided to 'go it alone' tested severely my elderly Agiflex shutter. Another factor which, of course, always had to be taken into account when photographing steam locomotives, was the strength and direction of the wind. On Shap the prevailing wind seemed to come from the west and more than one of my early morning pictures at Greenholme was marred by the exhaust blowing down at just the wrong moment. Equally well I recall one morning in early spring 1966 when a near gale force wind blowing from the east gave me some of my favourite Greenholme pictures. So fierce were conditions that day that no sooner had the exhaust left the locomotive's chimney than it would be snatched away by the wind to stream westwards across the countryside. On a sadder note, I also recall that on days when the rain never stopped and any form of worthwhile photography was impossible; it was at Greenholme that we used to sit in the car for hour after hour watching the trains go by in the gloom and listening ever hopefully to the weather forecasts on the wireless *(Plate x)*.

Although a steam-hauled train storming up Shap always made a dramatic picture, my favourite stretch of line for photography was from Grayrigg through Lowgill and the Lune Gorge to Tebay. Just south of Tebay, where the railway, road and river kept close company through the narrow entrance into the Lune Gorge, lay Dillicar troughs. Many were the happy hours I spent here, filming and photographing trains in extremely differing conditions. During my visit in April 1966 it was so cold one morning that water, splashed out of the troughs by passing trains, had frozen solid and the sleepers and paved gangers' walk at the side of the track were covered in a thick sheet of ice. Moving the heavy cine camera and tripod from one position to another became a precarious business and called for extreme caution. In complete contrast was a really gorgeous day in the following July when the temperature was up in the seventies. At the southern end of Dillicar troughs the ground rose sharply on the west side to form a ready-made grandstand and it was here, amidst clusters of foxgloves, that we settled down shortly after two thirty to watch the afternoon trains passing over the troughs. The only thing to spoil this idyllic spot was the noise of traffic on the road close by, but at least this kept me awake, counteracting the soporific effect of the hot sun and the intermittent droning of bees as they explored the foxgloves. There were not many freights that afternoon, but at about four thirty a 'Black Five' heading south with her train gave me my favourite picture from this spot *(Plate xvi)*.

The locations that I visited along the line between Oxenholme and Thrimby Grange must have been legion but none gave me so much pleasure as the Lune Gorge. Perhaps this was due in some part to the fact that I only went there when the weather was pleasant, for to reach my favourite spot entailed a walk up the line from Lowgill of about one and a half miles and the thought of being caught in the rain whilst doing this—and weighed down with heavy photographic equipment—was not exactly an attractive proposition. On 'Lune Gorge' days I would leave my car at the spot where Lowgill station used to be, but of which by 1965 no trace remained. Incidentally, right up to 1967 there were still signposts on the Kendal to Tebay road pointing to Grayrigg Station and Lowgill Station, both of which had long since ceased to exist. As Norman Lockett once remarked, what hard luck it would have been on a motorist who, his car having broken down, decided to walk the two miles to the railway to catch a train only to find on arrival that there was no station.

Our visits to the Lune Gorge were always made in the afternoon. We would arrive at Lowgill at about a quarter to one and after loading ourselves down with cameras, tripods and bags containing other bits of necessary equipment—including our picnic lunches—we would start walking. The aim was to reach our first location in the Lune Gorge at about the same time as the last of the procession of up diesel-hauled expresses passed by. About two hundred yards up the line from where I used to leave my car was Lowgill signal box and I always made a point of calling in and showing my photographic permit to the signalman on duty so that he would know that I had permission to be on company property. I got to know one of the signalmen quite well and used to look forward to seeing him again on each of my visits, for he was a very pleasant man and most helpful. Before each journey up to Westmorland I would write to my signalman friend saying when I was coming up and asking what turn of duty he would be on. I recall how surprised and sad I felt when, in answer to my letter early in 1967, he replied saying that he was no longer at Lowgill as the box had been demolished.

One of my happiest visits to the Lune Gorge was on 17 April 1967. It started off on an amusing note. We had been walking for about a mile and were approaching the spot where the line turned north when suddenly both of us saw it at the same moment—smoke rising above the bluff of hill behind which the line curved! Cine camera, tripod, picnic lunches etc, were hurriedly deposited on the ground and a mad scramble made up the side of the cutting to photograph the approaching train. Our rather breathless anticipation, however, was short-lived, for we soon realised that the smoke was not moving—it was, in fact, coming from a bonfire just lit by some gangers round the corner. Rather sheepishly, we climbed down the side of the cutting, gathered up our scattered equipment and started walking again, but we had not taken more than a few paces when a high pitched singing noise from the

xvi
91 NY 610023
". . . my favourite picture from this spot". Photographed on a hot summer's afternoon, 'Black Five' 4–6–0 No 44986 passes over the southern end of Dillicar troughs with an up freight. Today this grandstand on the lower slopes of Jeffery's Mount no longer exists: it was levelled and buried under masses of concrete for the M6 motorway. *16 July 1966.*

xvii
97 SD 923984
Coming into view around the bend at Dillicar Common near the southern end of the Lune Gorge, Stanier Class 5 4–6–0 No 45232 heads south towards Lowgill with an up freight. The track had recently been replaced with the continuous welded rail type, which gave a high pitched singing note heralding the approach of a train. *17 April 1967.*

xviii
97 SD 622990

"... one of those rare days when everything went right". Britannia class No 70022 *Tornado* is superbly captured by Ivo Peters' camera, running south through the Lune Gorge with an up freight.

As a small boy the writer well remembers his first sighting of *Tornado* soon after its allocation to the Western Region in 1951, for he was allowed on the footplate of this locomotive at Taunton, having waited at Exeter St David's to travel behind it on a northbound express, rather than catch an earlier train hauled by a Castle. Reward enough for one who was brought up to love only Swindon designed machines and who was totally in awe of this monster of alien proportions! *17 April 1967.*

continuous welded rail really *did* herald the approach of a train. Another unceremonious dumping of cine camera etc, and scramble up the bank ensued, to be rewarded this time by a southbound steam-hauled freight coming into view round the bend *(Plate xvii)*.

Unlike our grandstand spot overlooking Dillicar troughs, the Lune Gorge was very quiet. No sound of road traffic reached us, for the main road lay over a mile away. Nothing disturbed the peace of this warm spring afternoon except the occasional mournful cry of a curlew or the faint barking of a dog rounding up sheep on the far side of the gorge.

Gazing up into the sky, I was amused by the antics of a few small white clouds that were about. Instead of moving on a steady course, they were being caught in air currents eddying up from the fells and would move first this way and then that. Actually, from a photographic angle this was a bit worrying for just when one thought that a cloud was safely past the sun it would stop and then come drifting back again as if it was dancing the *Sir Roger de Coverley* with the sun! But 17 April 1967 was one of those rare days when everything went right: we were treated to a veritable procession of freights, all steam-hauled, and for all of them the sun shone *(Plate xviii)*. Perhaps it was fate being kind for although I did not know it at the time, this was to be the last occasion I would film steam in the Lune Gorge.

Now, not only has the steam locomotive gone, but so also has much of the peace and serenity of the Lune Gorge and Shap Fell for both have been terribly scarred by the construction of the M6 motorway.

Such is progress, but with how much happiness I remember the past. Perhaps it was for the best that I was destined never again to be able to visit my beloved Westmorland.

Ivo Peters BATH, 1987

FAREWELL, WESTMORLAND STEAM

The end of steam traction over Shap

Oxenholme

1 *(previous page)*
97 SD 530901
Fairburn 2–6–4T No 42154 leaves Oxenholme with a southbound local train. The station dates from 1846, being built by the Lancaster & Carlisle and Kendal & Windermere Railway companies, and is the junction for the Windermere branch. The layout has been considerably rationalised since the days of steam. The branch to Windermere, once double track, has been singled and now is only capable of DMU operation; however the platforms at Oxenholme have been extended, thus avoiding the need for expresses having to draw up twice. *24 April 1965.*

2
97 SD 532903
Taken the day before, 2–6–4T No 42154 sets off from Oxenholme for the Windermere branch. Once on the branch, the first two miles to Kendal were easy running, as the line was constructed on a falling gradient of 1:80. *23 April 1965.*

3

97 SD 532903

Fleetwood (10C) Stanier Class 5 No 45421 comes off the Windermere branch with an engineers' train and is about to gain the main line at the junction just north of Oxenholme station. Today the platforms of the station extend to where the engine is seen crossing the site of the former junction. *23 April 1965.*

4

97 SD 532906

The former layout is shown to good effect in this view looking south, taken in the fork of the junction just north of Oxenholme station, with Britannia No 70034 *Thomas Hardy* on the nine-coach 10.40am Euston–Carlisle train. The pure white exhaust of the Britannia Pacific is carried away by a typically strong prevailing westerly wind. The falling 1:80 gradient of the Windermere branch can be judged well on the right of this shot, although the main line is rising at 1:178. *23 April 1965.*

Docker Viaduct
5
97 SD 565956
Beautifully framed by Ivo's camera on a lovely autumn morning, an unidentified Stanier Class 5 makes a fine sight as it drifts down the gradient over Docker Viaduct and heads southwards towards Oxenholme with a long train of empty wagons. *20 October 1965.*

Grayrigg
6
97 SD 597960
Looking west from a small overbridge (No 89) near Grayrigg and observed approaching milepost 26 (from Lancaster), Stanier 'Black Five' 4–6–0 No 44915 from Lostock Hall shed (10D) rounds the bend with a northbound freight on the approach to the passing loops. In the last five years of its life, No 44915 was allocated to no fewer than four sheds before finally being stored at Carnforth in December 1967, prior to being scrapped in October 1968. *4 September 1965.*

7

97 SD 597960

Exactly the same location as the previous shot, but a totally different working: the Oxenholme banker Fairburn 2–6–4T No 42110 from Tebay, assists Jubilee 4–6–0 No 45627 *Sierra Leone* with a football special to Glasgow. Note the sloganised tender of the locomotive which has been 'zapped' by fans. The Jubilee was shedded at Bank Hall (8K), where it spent the last few months of its working life before being withdrawn the following September. *14 April 1966.*

8

97 SD 596960

As it passes under Bridge 89 carrying a minor road over the line, and from where the two previous shots were taken, the driver of Britannia Pacific No 70038 (formerly *Robin Hood*), from Carlisle Kingmoor MPD, keeps a careful eye on the train of wagons and pulls out of Grayrigg's up loop, having waited there for the passing of a diesel-hauled express. The Britannia has only two months to go before withdrawal from service. Note the home bracket signal on the left for the down loop. *16 June 1967.*

9

97 SD 597960

With mist shrouding the distant fells and steam in abundance on this damp autumn day, a literally atmospheric view is had from the road bridge looking east towards the former station at Grayrigg, the remains of which are still in evidence at this date. Britannia Pacific No 70011 *Hotspur*, minus its nameplates, hurries northwards with a down parcels train, whilst sister engine No 70025 *Western Star* waits in the up loop, also with a parcels train. One of No 70025's lamps seems to be somewhat askew and looks to be in danger of falling off! *15 October 1965.*

10

97 SD 598961

The Britannia's footplate crew seem to take an interest in Ivo's purpose to record its passing, as No 70032 (formerly *Tennyson*) with a northbound parcels train makes plenty of smoke as it climbs the last section of 1:106 on the approach to Grayrigg.

One of a second batch of twenty to be built (70025–44), No 70032 was fitted, as seen here, with a conventional tender. These differed from the high-sided 4,275-gallon, 9-ton capacity BR1D type fitted to the last batch of ten built, which had steam-operated coal pushers. The latter type was infinitely preferred by crews, as the streamlined design created a smoother airflow over the locomotive cab. The earlier model, although offering better rear view visibility, suffered from a back draught of air at speed, which caused swirling around the eaves of the roof, making the problem of airborne coal dust on the footplate much worse. However, during the last few months of its life, No 70032 was fitted with a BR1D type of tender taken from another of the class withdrawn earlier. *15 October 1965.*

11
97 SD 597960
With a clear road ahead, Liverpool Edge Hill (8A) 'Black Five' 4–6–0 No 45005 coasts downhill with a southbound freight. The photographer will not have to wait long for another train, as Grayrigg's down home signal is also off. *23 April 1965.*

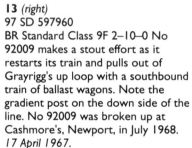

13 *(right)*
97 SD 597960
BR Standard Class 9F 2–10–0 No 92009 makes a stout effort as it restarts its train and pulls out of Grayrigg's up loop with a southbound train of ballast wagons. Note the gradient post on the down side of the line. No 92009 was broken up at Cashmore's, Newport, in July 1968. *17 April 1967.*

12
97 SD 597960
Here Carlisle Kingmoor (12A) shed BR 9F 2–10–0 No 92233 heads south with a train of motor car wagons. Changes are ever apparent from the same vantage point, not only in the moods of the weather, but also on the railway itself: the last remains of Grayrigg station, closed on 1 February 1954, have recently been swept away, leaving a scar on the down side of the line. The signal box finally closed in 1973 when power signalling replaced the semaphore types. *17 April 1967.*

14

97 SD 597960

The views to the distant Howgill, attracted Ivo to this particular location and was one of his favourites. The sun peeps through to highlight Langdale Fell, dominated by the 2,044ft peak of Fell Head seen in the left background, which forms a spectacular backdrop to Britannia Pacific No 70006 (formerly *Robert Burns*) making good progress in charge of an up freight, including a number of empty BICC cable drums. Note the ex-LNWR signals on the right. *14 July 1966.*

15

97 SD 597960

Britannia Class 7P No 70039 *Sir Christopher Wren*, shorn of its identification and deputising for a failed diesel, passes Grayrigg at speed with a Glasgow–Manchester express, whilst rebuilt Patriot Class 6P No 45531 awaits its passing in the up loop. *15 October 1965.*

16
97 SD 597960
This must be one of the most evocative shots taken in Westmorland by Ivo Peters. With storm clouds gathering over Langdale Fell, early morning sunlight catches rebuilt Patriot 4–6–0 No 45531 *Sir Frederick Harrison*, its nameplates already removed, pulling out of the up loop at Grayrigg on a humble freight duty, having waited for the passing of the Glasgow–Manchester express hauled by No 70039.

This photograph shows how passenger locomotives had fallen from grace in the twilight years of steam. The grubby external condition of the Patriot was perhaps indicative that it had not long to remain in service; in fact it was withdrawn only a month after this photograph was taken. No 45531 was broken up at Campbell's, Airdrie, between January and March 1966. *15 October 1965.*

Grayrigg loops
17
97 SD 602962
In the vivid fragrance of a spring evening of what had been a sullen day of drenching rain, Britannia Class 7P No 70005, the once-named *John Milton*, tops Grayrigg bank with a northbound freight and storms round the bend past the site of the former station. Working hard in the rear, the ubiquitous Fairburn 2–6–4T No 42210 is about to drop off after giving banking assistance from Oxenholme. *17 April 1967.*

18

97 SD 602961

On a dull and overcast day a faithful workhorse is photographed in full cry: working very hard with an impressive exhaust blasting from its chimney, Stanier Class 5 4–6–0 No 44672 from Carlisle Kingmoor shed, storms round the bend past Grayrigg box unassisted with a northbound parcels train on the main line. The former stationmaster's house is just visible in the background through the smoke over the train. *24 April 1965.*

19

97 SD 603961

His engine having elevated its train from Oxenholme unassisted, the fireman of BR Class 9F 2–10–0 No 92096 leans out of the cab to take a breather. Soon he will have some hard firing to do on the final assault of Shap, just a few miles further north; but the train will halt at Tebay where a 2–6–4T banker will render assistance to the summit. *21 September 1966.*

20

97 SD 603961

Unlike freight workings, when a northbound parcels train required a banker, the usual practice was for one of the Oxenholme 2–6–4 tanks to couple ahead of the train engine and assist all the 18 miles to Shap Summit. Although their exhausts would signify otherwise, Stanier Class 5 No 45109 and Fairburn 2–6–4T No 42210 made light work of the northbound parcels train as they topped Grayrigg bank on a bright summer's morning. *16 July 1966.*

21

97 SD 603961

Fitted with a snowplough under its buffer beam, Stanier Class 5 4–6–0 No 44795 passes Grayrigg with a down freight. Once again Ivo's activities have caught the attention of a locomotive's footplate crew: the 'Black Five's' fireman seems quite content to 'pose' for the camera and is recorded for posterity! Withdrawn three months later, No 44795 did not survive the year and was broken up at McWilliam's, Shettleston, in December. *28 April 1967.*

22
97 SD 604962
On a fine sunny morning, with its fireman 'taking the air', BR Britannia Pacific No 70025 (formerly *Western Star*), going well, passes by at speed with a down parcels train. BR Class 9F 2–10–0 No 92019 has been diverted into the loop and waits with an oil train. Note the two box vans fitted as barrier wagons. *16 July 1966.*

23
97 SD 605962
Having waited for Britannia class No 70025 to pass with its northbound parcels train, BR Class 9F 2–10–0 No 92019 gets the road at last and sets off north with its oil train. This view not only clearly shows the loops at Grayrigg, but also the two barrier wagons behind the locomotive's tender and the one placed ahead of the guard's van. *16 July 1966.*

24
97 SD 603961
Tebay (12E) Ivatt Class 4MT 2–6–0 No 43029 is busy propelling ballast wagons into the yard at Grayrigg. The fireman keeps an eye open and watches the guard's reversing instructions as he directs the footplate crew from a position standing on the front ballast wagon. *16 July 1966.*

25

97 SD 603961

Chester shed (6A) ex-LMS Class 8F 2–8–0 No 48723, emitting a fine plume of pure white exhaust, passes the loops at Grayrigg with an empty freight of vans and bogie bolsters. The 8F survived until the end of BR steam, being withdrawn in August 1968 and was cut up at Ward's, Beighton, Sheffield, in December of that year. *21 September 1966.*

26

97 SD 604962

Having pulled into the down loop with a northbound freight, the fireman of Carlisle Kingmoor Stanier Class 5 4–6–0 No 44937 takes the opportunity to get some coal forward from the tender before the train resumes its journey. The 'Black Five' had only a matter of active days left and was withdrawn from service only a week or two later. *28 April 1967.*

27
97 SD 604962
With the signals off and a clear road ahead, Stanier 'Black Five' No 45198, running south with an up freight, is about to traverse the crossover at the eastern end of the loops. The locomotive carries the 8F shed code denoting that it is from Springs Branch, Wigan, to which it was allocated only the month before; No 45198 was withdrawn the following July.
28 April 1967.

28
97 SD 604962
Devoid of its 12A shed plate, Stanier Class 5 4–6–0 No 45455, which has been fitted with a snowplough, heads south with a permanent way train. The overbridge in the background carries a minor road. Today the M6 cuts diagonally across the line on a wide bridge almost where Ivo Peters was standing to take this and several other views of Grayrigg's loops.
28 April 1967.

29
97 SD 604962
Ex-LMS Class 8F 2–8–0 No 48528 from Edge Hill shed passes the loops with a
down freight, mainly consisting of tanker wagons. No 48528 was withdrawn in
August 1967 and scrapped at Buttigieg's, Newport, in December of that year.
16 July 1966.

53

30
97 SD 604962
With an impressive exhaust rising well above its train, Britannia class No 70050 *Firth of Clyde*, from Crewe North (5A) shed, accelerates past the loops with a northbound freight, whilst its fireman looks out of the cab at an injector pipe which is draining onto the track.

No 70050 ended its days at Carlisle Kingmoor (12A) until its withdrawal in August 1966. Being one of the Britannias fitted with high-sided tenders with a larger capacity, thus requiring less servicing; it spent a short period of time shedded at Banbury (2D) from September 1965 to work passenger semi-fasts on the ex-GC main line, which by then had few depot facilities left open to service them. *24 April 1965.*

31
97 SD 605962
With only a matter of days to go before withdrawal, Royal Scot 4–6–0 No 46160 (formerly *Queen Victoria's Rifleman*) on a down part fitted freight, has a clear road past Grayrigg's loops, having left its banker further round the bend. The locomotive was cut up by the Motherwell Machinery & Scrap Co Wishaw, in the following July. *24 April 1965.*

32
97 SD 605962
The footplate crew of Stanier 4MT 2–6–4T No 42665, waiting in the down loop
prior to returning to Oxenholme for another banking duty, watches the passing
of Britannia No 70049 *Solway Firth*, already shorn of its nameplates, on an up
fitted freight. The fireman of the Pacific has spotted Ivo Peters standing by the
lineside and adopts a suitable pose for the camera. No 70049 was one of the last
batch of Britannias built in 1954 at Crewe, but was not named until May 1959.
22 September 1966.

33
97 SD 605962
Going really well as judged by the smoke 'wave' ahead of its funnel, Carlisle
Kingmoor Britannia Class 7P No 70033 *Charles Dickens*, deprived of its
identification, storms past Grayrigg in charge of a down parcels train. *15 July
1966.*

34

97 SD 604962

With the Howgills forming a magnificent backcloth, BR Class 9F 2–10–0 No 92249 from Carlisle Kingmoor shed passes the signals at the end of Grayrigg's down loop running light engine and tender first, whilst Angela O'Shea, standing on the right, captures the moment on colour film. The overbridge in the background has since been demolished with the advent of the M6 motorway and has been replaced with a tunnel-like concrete structure over the line. Note what appears to be the roof of Ivo Peters' Bentley just visible over the parapet of the bridge. *30 July 1965.*

35

97 SD 607962

The driver of ex-Crosti 9F 2–10–0 No 92021 keeps a sharp eye open for the signal, as he is about to be diverted into the up loop at Grayrigg to await the passing of an express working. The loops at Grayrigg were shortened in the late 1960s, as can be gauged from this shot looking back through the small overbridge at the eastern end, which shows newly laid and ballasted track on the down side; the points used to be under the bridge, as observed in the previous view. *7 August 1967.*

Summer Saturday extras and football specials at Grayrigg
(By 1965 all regular expresses were diesel-hauled)

36
97 SD 604962
Carnforth shedded ex-LMS Class 5 No 45445 passes Grayrigg with a Saturdays-only express from Blackpool to Glasgow. The fireman's knotted handkerchief worn as protective headgear suggests he would be suitably apparelled for the beach at Blackpool and it begs the question whether his trousers were also rolled up on this hot summer's day! *16 July 1966.*

37
97 SD 603961
BR Britannia Pacific No 70013 (ex-*Oliver Cromwell*) passes Grayrigg signal box at speed with the 9.30am Saturdays-only Blackpool–Glasgow service. No 70013 is one of the two Britannias preserved and now resides at Bressingham Gardens, Diss, Norfolk. The other member of the class preserved is No 70000 *Britannia.* *16 July 1966.*

38
97 SD 597960
The now-preserved Royal Scot Class 7P 4–6–0 No 46115 *Scots Guardsman* is spotted at Grayrigg during its final months in BR service hauling a Glasgow–Liverpool express. It was withdrawn in December at Carlisle Kingmoor. At the time of writing, the locomotive resides at the Birmingham Railway Museum's Tyseley depot awaiting restoration to running order. *30 July 1965.*

39
97 SD 604962
As 5B Crewe (South) Stanier 'Black Five' No 45353 heads north past Grayrigg's loop signals with the 10.45am (SO) Blackpool–Dundee service, the fireman keeps an eye on the passengers, freshly suntanned after a holiday by the sea, as they hang out of carriage windows taking advantage of the cooling breeze on a hot summer's day. *12 August 1967.*

40

97 SD 605962

Having been halted in the down loop to await the passage of an express, Stanier Class 5 4–6–0 No 45395 from 8A Springs Branch (Wigan) shed sets off from Grayrigg with a Liverpool–Glasgow football special. Fans have chalked the projected score of the match on the 'Black Five's' smokebox door; they were a little optimistic, for Liverpool lost to Celtic 1–0 in the away match. However Liverpool had their revenge in the return leg winning 2–0, so in the end they won 2–1 on aggregate! *14 April 1966.*

41

97 SD 604962

Carlisle Upperby (12B) BR Britannia Pacific No 70032 (ex-*Tennyson*) speeds north towards the border with the 10.45am (SO) Blackpool to Edinburgh train. Upperby closed at the end of the year and the Britannia was transferred to 12A Kingmoor shed. *16 July 1966.*

Cowperthwaite
42
97 SD 610965
Taken a year earlier, Britannia class No 70032 *Tennyson*, then recently deprived of
its identity, rounds the bend at Cowperthwaite with a down freight on the
approach to Lowgill and the junction with the ex-LNW Sedbergh–Ingleton–
Clapham line. The driver keeps a lookout for Lowgill's down home signals, which
undoubtedly will be in his favour, judging by the locomotive's speed. *29 July 1965.*

Beck Foot Viaduct
43
97 SD 617967
Ivatt Class 4MT 2–6–0 No 43017 crosses the elegant Beck Foot (or Lowgill) Viaduct on the disused Ingleton line, which had closed a year earlier but was used for the dumping of spent ballast. The signalman at Lowgill tipped off Ivo about this working; the Ivatt had been down to Sedbergh to collect some empty ballast wagons and is caught coming back over the viaduct towards Lowgill with its train.

No 43017 is of interest to Somerset & Dorset aficionados, since the locomotive, together with Nos 43013 and 43036, worked the West Country route for a period in 1949/50. The Ivatt 2–6–0s were not a success on the steeply-graded line: although then fitted with double blastpipe and chimney, they were poor steamers and generally disliked by S&D enginemen, who disparagingly named them 'Doodlebugs'! *29 July 1965*.

Lowgill

44 *(left, above)*

97 SD 622970

Britannia Pacific No 70018 *Flying Dutchman*, wearing what appears to be unofficially made nameplates on the smoke deflectors, passes by with a southbound mixed freight. In the foreground is the ex-LNW branch that diverged from the main line at Lowgill to run down the Lune Valley through Sedbergh, Ingleton and the 'other' Clapham Junction. Today the formation of the branch near the old junction is covered with trees, mainly silver birch. *14 April 1966.*

45 *(left, below)*

97 SD 622971

At 7.00am on a crisp autumn day, 5B Crewe (South) shed Class 5 No 44832 speeds past Lowgill box with an up fitted freight, leaving behind a long trail of white exhaust in the still morning air, the driver having pulled his cap well down over his forehead to prevent it being blown off. Closed on 7 March 1960, by this date Lowgill station had already been demolished and when Ivo visited the area a year later the signal box had also suffered the same fate. *21 September 1966.*

46

97 SD 621971

In a scene to delight the steam enthusiast, but much to the chagrin of the diesel fan, Britannia No 70006 (ex-*Robert Burns*) hauls a failed Brush Type 4 diesel-electric, No D1845 (Class 47 TOPS No 47195, named *Muricidae* in September 1988), then just four months old, past the site of the former station at Lowgill and heads north towards Carlisle and the Lune Gorge just round the bend. Condemned in November 1991, at the time of writing No 47195 is awaiting disposal at Tinsley TMD. *4 September 1965.*

47

97 SD 622972

Patricroft (9H) BR Caprotti Class 5 4–6–0 No 73140, with a southbound fitted freight, passes the up home signals for Lowgill Junction. The slopes in the right background form part of Fell Head on Langdale Fell, whilst those on the left are on Dillicar Common. *14 April 1966.*

48

97 SD 622972

By contrast, and in no particular hurry, 5B Crewe (South) Britannia No 70023 *Venus* saunters southwards past the junction at Lowgill with an up parcels train. Today the M6 motorway has been carved out of the fellside behind the locomotive, totally transforming this scene. *14 April 1966.*

Dillicar Common
49
97 SD 622976
A fine photograph that captures perfectly the beauty of the Cumbrian countryside through which the West Coast main line runs. With Carlin Gill separating the 1,745 ft Uldale Head from the north-western slopes of Fell Head, along which the Roman-built Fairmile Road traverses, an imposing backdrop is formed to the now-preserved Britannia class No 70013 *Oliver Cromwell*, seen in charge of an up empty wagon train, as it trundles round the bend just north of Lowgill at the southern end of the Lune Gorge.

It befell No 70013 to work the last steam-hauled passenger train over Shap: a football supporters' special which left Carlisle at 9.45am on 26 December 1967. The locomotive was specially prepared and cleaned for the occasion by a dedicated group of enthusiasts, the Master Neverer's Association (MNA), at 12A Carlisle (Kingmoor) depot. The MNA was responsible for many such activities in the last days of steam and ensured that its beloved locomotives looked at their best, particularly when working farewell or enthusiasts' specials—and often just before being consigned to the scrap heap. Judging from the Britannia's fair condition in this view, when only a thin coat of grime veils its paintwork, the task cannot have been too onerous. *12 August 1967.*

50

97 SD 623985

Stanier Class 5 No 45048, in a very grubby state which all but obscures its cabside number, and Britannia Pacific No 70031, formerly *Byron*, head round the bend at the southern end of the Lune Gorge with a heavy northbound parcels train. Both locomotives were to be withdrawn by the end of the year: No 45048, from 8F Springs Branch (Wigan) shed, was broken up at Draper's, Hull, in February 1968, whilst No 70031 met its end at McWilliam's, Shettleston, in March 1968. *28 April 1967.*

51

97 SD 623985

The background dominated by Blease Fell, the summit of which is 1,555ft above mean sea level, 8A Edge Hill depot Stanier Class 5 4–6–0 No 44964 with an up goods, heads south from the Lune Gorge towards Lowgill. The course of the River Lune runs through the valley immediately behind the locomotive and almost parallel to the line at this point. In the middle distance is the ravine of Carlin Gill which now forms the north-western boundary of the Yorkshire Dales National Park. *21 September 1966.*

52
97 SD 623985
Taken on a gloriously sunny evening from a position a few yards further north round the bend, with the farmstead of Low Carlingill nestling at the foot of Blease Fell in view, Class 5 4–6–0 No 45048, having worked a down parcels train with Britannia No 70031 earlier in the day, looms into view with a southbound freight of vans. The locomotive has about seven months of operational life left: withdrawn in November, it was finally scrapped in February 1968 at Draper's, Hull. *28 April 1967.*

The Lune Gorge
53
97 SD 621990
The magnificence of the Lune Gorge can be judged fully in this aspect of it looking north towards Tebay from Ivo Peters' perch on the bluff on the west side of the line. Carlisle Kingmoor Stanier Class 5 4–6–0 No 45295 drifts southwards through the gorge with an up empty ballast train; the winding course of the River Lune adds to the glorious setting. *17 April 1967.*

54

97 SD 621990

Taken from the same commanding view a little later and—at first glance—of an identical working, Stanier Class 5 No 45135 heads south with an empty coal train. It is apparent from his relaxed posture that the splendour of the gorge is not lost on the 'Black Five's' fireman who is enjoying taking in the area's classic topography, although he has probably been through it hundreds of times before. The fell in the middle background is Jeffery's Mount, under which Dillicar troughs are located, whilst the western slopes of Blease Fell are on the right of the picture. *17 April 1967.*

55

97 SD 621990

It is easy to understand how Ivo Peters was at one with the world during his visits to the Lune Gorge with its tranquillity and impressive scenery. On this day, as with others, he lingered here for some time to record the passage of several trains through it. On this occasion Britannia class No 70032 (ex-*Tennyson*) is running south with a special freight of pipes. It is rather ironic to think that BP has recently constructed a major ethylene pipeline from Grangemouth to the Merseyside area, which now runs underground through the Lune Gorge; but once the re-landscaping is complete it will be undetectable. By way of contrast, the M6 which runs close to the western side of the line here would have robbed Ivo of his vantage point, as the motorway's southbound carriageway now carves through the spot. *17 April 1967.*

56
97 SD 621990
Looking down from the bluff on Dillicar Common and seen rounding the bend heading north with a freight, Carlisle Kingmoor 'Black Five' No 44900, with barely nine months to go before withdrawal, saunters through the gorge towards Dillicar troughs, some two miles away. The driver adopts a relaxed pose and leans nonchalantly from the cab whilst he seemingly is absorbing the tranquil atmosphere of the Lune Gorge. The locomotive was put to the cutter's torch in November 1967. *21 September 1966.*

57
97 SD 622991
A splendid aspect is had from track level of BR Standard Class 9F 2–10–0 No 92056 running north with a banana train as it rounds a bluff in the Lune Gorge from which Ivo Peters took many of his best photographs. This was a perfect spring day, when nothing disturbed the peace except for the occasional cry of a curlew or the distant barking of a dog rounding-up sheep on the far side of the gorge. The bluff on Dillicar Common was decapitated during the construction of the M6 motorway, which runs very close to this point and from which the noise is incessant. Gibbet Hill on the western slopes of Langdale Fell is on the left of the picture and fortunately remains the same. *17 April 1967.*

58
91 NY 610017
Seen approaching Low Borrowbridge towards the northern end of the Lune
Gorge, and where there was a Roman fort, ex-LMS Class 5 4–6–0 No 45118,
fitted with a snowplough, drifts round the bend with a down train of empty coal
wagons and nears Dillicar troughs, where it will top-up its water supply before
the assault of Shap commences. A good view is to be had of Birk Knott towering
1,270ft AMSL behind the train. *14 April 1966.*

Dillicar troughs

59

91 NY 610024

Having been put into the up loop at Tebay to allow an express to pass, Stanier 'Black Five' No 45210, with its cabside and smokebox number all but obscured, making positive identification uncertain even on this bright autumn day, gets to grips with its train of covered wagons but is still going too slowly over the troughs to pick up water. Judging by the locomotive's exhaust a lot of firing is going on, but the next few miles will be easy running, demanding no great effort from the crew. *19 October 1965.*

60

91 NY 612026

An early morning shot: the ever-present Carlisle Kingmoor BR Standard Class 9F 2–10–0 No 92019 in charge of an up freight takes water as it passes over the northern end of Dillicar troughs. The bridge in the background carried the A685 road over the line; with the advent of the motorway, it was demolished to make way for a concrete structure that spans both it, the M6 and the railway at this point. *15 July 1966.*

61
91 NY 610025
The meadow in the foreground abutting the A685 road is a good vantage point for Ivo to record 6B Mold Junction Stanier 'Black Five' No 44917 in charge of a mixed down freight, and taking water as it passes over Dillicar troughs. The steep slopes of Brockholes Bank on Tebay Fell rise above the wooded banks of the River Lune, with Low Borrowbridge visible in the middle distance over the train. This same aspect would be somewhat tricky to achieve today, as one would be standing on the southbound carriageway of the M6! *29 July 1965.*

A vanishing scene: Britannias replenishing aplenty!
62
91 NY 612025
With the shadowy north face of the 1,325ft-high Birk Knott in the distance brooding over the scene, Britannia Pacific No 70013 *Oliver Cromwell*, now preserved, passes over the water troughs at Dillicar, takes advantage of its speed thereby ensuring the water supply is amply replenished, as it heads north with a down summer Saturday relief working. The A685 main road runs behind the stone wall at the foot of Jeffery's Mount on the extreme right of the picture; today the M6 passes between the line and the re-aligned road. *12 August 1967.*

84

63

91 NY 612025

The epitome of power and speed: as if on a final fling before oblivion, Britannia Pacific No 70010 *Owen Glendower*, recently deprived of its nameplates and in a very shabby state, storms over Dillicar troughs with the 8.25am (SO) Morecombe–Glasgow express. The smoke wave obscuring its funnel would suggest the locomotive is travelling at least 70mph. Withdrawn from service at Kingmoor Carlisle depot very soon after this photograph was taken, No 70010 was reduced to scrap at McWilliam's, Shettleston, in January 1968. *12 August 1967.*

64

91 NY 612025

By way of contrast to the previous shot, Britannia 7P No 70027 *Rising Star*, still in absolutely pristine condition soon after being outshopped from Crewe Works following an overhaul, heads south with an up parcels train and takes on water as it passes over Dillicar troughs. Besides taking this photograph, Ivo was also filming the locomotive and had great fears of getting a soaking, but they were unfounded and instead he was treated to a spectacular rainbow as the train passed by. *20 October 1965.*

Lune's Bridge, Tebay
65
91 NY 613028
Viewed from the main A685 road bridge spanning the line adjacent to Lune's Bridge, Stanier Class 5 4–6–0 No 45209 from Carnforth (10A) shed heads south with an up freight and crosses the River Lune on Bridge 106, having just passed through Tebay station some few hundred yards further north. Note the bridge's number mounted on a signpost near the parapet on the down side of the line.
14 April 1966.

Greenholme
66
91 NY 602059
The curvature of the line together with the fine panoramic views at Greenholme afforded the photographer the chance of obtaining some memorable shots. Ivo, being no exception, took full advantage of the location and obtained this superb study of Britannia Pacific No 70025 (ex-*Western Star*) climbing well unassisted on a short northbound freight. The Tebay and Langdale fells on the Howgills stand out clearly on this lovely spring evening; the passage of the Lune Gorge is sandwiched between them and Grayrigg Common, seen on the right over the train. The village of Tebay is on the left in the middle distance. *28 April 1967.*

67
91 NY 602057
Pounding up the 1:75 climb to Greenholme unassisted, Britannia class No 70028
(ex-*Royal Star*), with a northbound parcels train, makes good progress at about
the halfway point on the long climb to Shap Summit from Tebay. The Howgills
can just be made out in the distance on this fairly hazy and cloudy day. *13 July
1966.*

68

91 NY 602059

In the beginning: on a gloriously sunny but chilly spring evening with long shadows casting their mantle over the foreground and sheep grazing undisturbed in the field beyond, Carlisle Kingmoor Stanier Class 5 4–6–0 No 45126, still with steam to spare, heads a northbound freight as it climbs hard towards Scotchman's Bridge at Greenholme. Note Ivo's friend, Norman Lockett, standing under the tree on the right. It was generally his photographic style to get as close as possible to the subjects, therefore he often appeared in Ivo's photographs, rather like artist Terence Cuneo's mouse . . . some mouse! *21 April 1966.*

69

91 NY 602059

And at the end: working hard at the rear of the train, an unidentified Fairburn 2–6–4T, probably No 42210, assists Class 5 No 45126 with its train of vans on the climb from Tebay, set far in the valley below and behind the pall of smoke. An everlasting memory of steam over Shap was the way trains heralded their approach long before they came into view: their communicating whistles at the commencement of the climb from Tebay broke the silence and then columns of smoke could be seen arising high in the air as they started out from the station area. *21 April 1966.*

70
91 NY 602057
Judging by the black smoke from its exhaust, some firing is taking place as Carlisle Kingmoor shed Stanier 'Black Five' 4–6–0 No 45135 elevates a northbound freight and passes the linesman's hut on the climb to Greenholme. The Class 5 had only two months left in service, being withdrawn in October and broken up at McWilliam's, Shettleston, in March 1968; the hut, however, survives today. *11 August 1967.*

71
91 NY 603058
With the driver's hair blown flat by the wind, Britannia Pacific No 70024 *Vulcan*, devoid of its nameplates, speeds under Scotchman's Bridge at Greenholme with a southbound parcels train and swiftly descends the 1:75 gradient towards Tebay, some three miles below. Norman Lockett stands on the embankment to get a slightly higher view, whilst the roof of Ivo's midnight-blue Bentley is just visible parked on the bridge. *28 April 1967.*

72
91 NY 602059
With low cloud covering the tops of the Howgill Fells in the distance, Stanier Class 5 No 45109, from 8B Warrington shed, climbs up towards Greenholme with a five-coach Warrington to Carlisle train, whilst a filthy and unidentified Fairburn Class 4 2–6–4T returns downhill to Tebay for another turn of duty, having banked a freight to Shap Summit. The three-arch Birkbeck Viaduct can be just made out in the background over the 'Black Five'. *15 April 1965.*

73
91 NY 602060
One of the last remaining ex-Crosti 9F 2–10–0s, No 92024, from Birkenhead (8H) depot, climbing well with a northbound train of empty bogie wagons, approaches Scotchman's Bridge at Greenholme. Ample assistance is being rendered by a Tebay 2–6–4T, which can just be made out through the smoke at the rear of the train. No 92024 would be withdrawn before the end of the year, finally succumbing to the cutter's torch in May 1968. *16 June 1967.*

74

91 NY 601059

An interesting working is captured on camera on a clear autumn evening: with a cotton-white exhaust signifying little effort, Warrington (8B) Standard Class 9F No 92160 climbs towards Greenholme with an engineers' train and hurries northwards, to where it is required for an undisclosed task. *19 October 1965.*

75

91 NY 602059

On a hazy summer's day, Britannia No 70005, formerly *John Milton*, then just a month away from withdrawal, is seen working hard to elevate a northbound freight towards Greenholme, with assistance being rendered by an unidentified Standard Class 4 4–6–0 from Tebay shed. Of some amusement are the hens scratching about in the field on the left, totally unmoved by the roaring and snorting iron monster over the wall! *16 June 1967.*

Scout Green

77

91 NY 596080

The line continues to climb from Greenholme at 1:75 on a mile-long embankment towards Scout Green. Standing near a minor road on the east side of the line not more than 100yd from the signal box, Ivo Peters had a grandstand view of trains as they tackled the section. Here ex-LMS Class 5 4–6–0 No 45120, assisted in the rear by a 2–6–4T, climbs towards Shap with a northbound freight. The visibility is good on this warm summer's day, offering a clear view to the distant fells and the Lune Gorge, seen in the middle of the picture. *14 July 1966.*

76

91 NY 602059

With steam to spare and an impressive exhaust suggesting the fireman is certainly earning his bread and butter, Stanier Class 8F 2–8–0 No 48211 from 10D Lostock Hall shed rounds the bend on the approach to Scotchman's Bridge at Greenholme on a misty autumn day. *15 October 1965.*

78
91 NY 596080
A very similar working photographed on a day when the visibility was not quite so good, although infinitely preferable to the bleak conditions often experienced on Shap. Here an unidentified Stanier Class 5, with an impressive exhaust accentuated by the chilly conditions and an emission of steam from an injector pipe, which appears to have blown back, slogs up the gradient towards Scout Green signal box. A trusty Tebay 2–6–4T renders help in the titanic struggle to elevate this heavy train, mainly consisting of tanker wagons, to Shap Summit.

Today the area in the foreground has been re-landscaped dramatically and the same vantage point would almost be abutting the northbound carriageway of the M6 motorway, albeit constructed much higher above the line than this elevation shows. *22 April 1967.*

79 *(right, above)*
91 NY 596080
On a lovely bright morning, with the Shap Fells standing out clearly in the background, Britannia Class 7P No 70048 *The Territorial Army 1908–1958*, bereft of nameplates, descends from Scout Green with a southbound parcels train. The roof of the signal box is just visible over the train to the left of the trees, which survive to this day. *14 July 1966.*

80 *(right, below)*
91 NY 596080
By way of contrast to the previous shot, this photograph serves to illustrate the changing weather moods on Shap. On a misty morning Stanier Class 5 4–6–0 No 45431 climbs the 1:75 gradient towards Shap at Scout Green with a northbound freight, assisted as usual by one of the Tebay 2–6–4Ts. No 45431 was broken up at Draper's, Hull in May 1968. *22 April 1965.*

81

91 NY 593081

The tiny signal box at Scout Green is portrayed well in this misty early morning shot showing an unidentified Stanier Class 5 4–6–0, possibly Carnforth-shedded No 44758, unassisted, approaching the crossing with a down parcels train. The 5½ mile climb, much of it at 1:75, from Tebay to Shap Summit was such a potential bottleneck, that it was divided into no fewer than four block sections northbound, with intermediate colour-light signals at Tebay North (Greenholme) and Shap Wells. Between them the diminutive box at Scout Green controlled the crossing, its own four signals and those of Shap Wells' IB. *22 April 1965.*

82

91 NY 594081

With a summer storm brewing over the fells, Stanier Class 5 No 45187 from 8A Edge Hill (Liverpool) shed, assisted by a 2–6–4T in the rear, thunders past Scout Green box with a northbound freight and heads towards Shap Summit, some 2½ miles away. The box was demolished in 1973 on commissioning of the power signalling system, but the colour-light on the up side of the line was installed in June 1963, some ten years earlier. With the advent of the M6, the crossing was closed; today it is no more and the gate on the up side is replaced by a stone wall. *28 July 1965.*

Salterwath
83
91 NY 584094
Standing on the west side of the line at Salterwath, an isolated farmstead between Scout Green and Shap, gave a worm's eye view of trains passing by on an embankment a mile or so from the summit. Here snowplough-fitted Class 5 No 45120, from 12A Carlisle (Kingmoor) depot, climbs steadily uphill with a northbound freight. *15 April 1965.*

84 *(right, above)*
91 NY 584094
With its grubby state making identification impossible, a Fairburn 2–6–4T assists Class 5 No 45259, in charge of a down freight, on the final section from Salterwath towards Shap Summit, which is located a few hundred yards north beyond the rock cutting just visible on the left of the picture. The dry stone walling is very much part of the fell landscape; a dearth of trees and hedgerows made photography somewhat easier. *15 April 1965.*

85 *(right, below)*
91 NY 583094
A unique Stanier Class 5 spotted at Salterwath: No 44767 with a Warrington–Kingmoor goods, pounds towards the summit at Shap. Of the 842 'Black Fives' built, this was the only one of its class to have Stephenson's valve gear fitted. Although withdrawn from BR service in December 1967 after some twenty years of operation, by good fortune No 44767 survives today and is preserved on the North Yorkshire Moors Railway, being appropriately named *George Stephenson*. *23 April 1965.*

Shap Wells (Ivo Peters' 'Classic' location)
86
91 NY 580100
With an impressive pall of black smoke issuing from its chimney, Stanier 'Black Five' No 45236, with a northbound freight, labours up the final few hundred yards to the summit past Shap Wells. This location was one of Ivo's favourites, which he and Norman Lockett dubbed 'Classic'. Being very near to the Shap Wells Hotel, it was a convenient spot for early morning or after dinner shots to be taken, which only required a few minutes' walk.

Stanier No 45236 was withdrawn four months later in December and cut up at Wards, Inverkeithing in April 1968. *7 August 1967.*

87
91 NY 580100
The crew of Carlisle Upperby (12B) Britannia Pacific No 70018 *Flying Dutchman*, with chalked or paper nameplates on its smoke deflectors, have spotted Ivo photographing the locomotive, which was working very hard with a Fairburn 2–6–4T in the rear, as it passes Shap Wells with a down freight. Withdrawn the following December, No 70018 did not survive the end of steam and was broken up by the Motherwell Machinery & Scrap Co, Wishaw, in June 1967.

Salterwath Cottages, now demolished, can be seen beyond the train and to the right of the picture. The rear driveway to the Shap Wells Hotel, accessed from the Orton–Shap road, passes under the line (Bridge 116) just out of sight beyond the first clump of bushes growing on the embankment near the telegraph pole. *14 July 1966.*

88

91 NY 580100

A ghostly apparition? Seen in the late afternoon, with a strong westerly wind blowing its black exhaust away from the line, a BR 9F 2–10–0, believed to be No 92093, and going very well, blasts up past Shap Wells with a bulk ammonia train, assisted by Standard Class 4 4–6–0 No 75037—then based at 12E Tebay shed.

The grubby state of the 9F caused Ivo to misidentify it as No 92033, which was withdrawn two years earlier in September 1965 from Northampton (1H) depot and scrapped at Ward's, Killamarsh, the following December. Shedded at Carlisle Kingmoor, No 92093 was withdrawn in the same month as this shot was taken, so it is just possible that it was the photographic subject on this occasion. No 92093 was broken up by the Motherwell Machinery & Scrap Co, Wishaw, in February 1968. *11 August 1967.*

89

91 NY 580100

The tranquillity of Shap is summed up perfectly in this shot with the distant Howgills bathed in evening sunlight, showing why Ivo chose the name 'Classic' for this location. Looking in remarkably clean condition, Stanier Class 5 4–6–0 No 45450, from 10D Lostock Hall depot, has rather a struggle with a bulk cement train as it nears the summit. The gruelling northbound climb of the four-mile section at 1:75 from Tebay, which always presented such a challenge to enginemen since the line's inception, is nearly over; not only for No 45450, but in every sense of the word, for in a few months, with the end of the steam era, modern traction would obviate the need for bankers and rob the observer of spectacles such as this. Tebay (12E) shed, the home of the bankers, would close to steam traction from 1 January 1968.

The area in the immediate foreground has now been planted with conifer trees, so this aspect is also no longer available to the would-be photographer. Despite its external condition, the 'Black Five' was withdrawn three months later, and was scrapped at Cashmore's, Great Bridge, in February 1968. *11 August 1967.*

90
91 NY 580100
Taken earlier on the same day as the previous two shots when the clouds blotted out the sun and haze all but obscured the distant fells, Stanier Class 5 4–6–0 No 45310, from 8F Springs Branch, Wigan, gets assistance from a Tebay Standard Class 4 with a long northbound freight up past Shap Wells. The Stanier survived until August 1968 and was eventually scrapped by Cohen's, Cargo Fleet, Middlesbrough, in December 1968. *11 August 1967.*

91
91 NY 579102
At 916ft above sea level Shap Summit was the high point of the ex-LNWR route from the English lowlands to the Scottish border, just north of Carlisle. Edge Hill (8A) depot Stanier Class 5 4–6–0 No 45069, in charge of an up freight, drifts through the rock cutting down from the summit, which was marked by a maroon-painted sign noting the elevation, beyond the steel footbridge in the background. *13 July 1966.*

92
91 NY 578102
Class 5 4–6–0 No 44677 coasts downhill from the summit and past Shap Wells with a southbound freight. In the background on Hardendale Fell is the isolated house at Beck Head, which stands surrounded by its protective shield of trees—vital because of the bleak conditions often experienced here. *22 September 1966.*

93
91 NY 579102
Looking as if it has recently emerged from a works overhaul, Stanier 'Black Five' 4–6–0 No 45330, from 8L Aintree depot, heads south with an up freight through the cutting at Shap Wells. By this date it was rare to see locomotives in such immaculate condition. No 45330 survived until the end of steam and was withdrawn in August 1968, but did not see in the New Year, being cut up at Cashmore's, Newport, in December. *13 July 1966.*

Hardendale
94
90 NY 568125
About to pass under the B6261 road bridge near Hardendale, Stanier Jubilee Class 6P 4–6–0 No 45698 *Mars*, speeds northwards from Shap Summit with a Liverpool–Glasgow relief working. The main A6 road runs behind the stone wall on the right, beyond which is Low Fell. The Jubilee from Bank Hall (8K) shed was withdrawn some seven months later and broken up at Ward's, Beighton, in February 1966. *15 April 1965.*

95
90 NY 568128
Passing the quarry sidings on the east side of the main line at Hardendale, Stanier Class 5 No **44886**, from Carlisle Kingmoor depot, leaving a fine exhaust plume in its wake and with steam to spare, approaches the B6261 road bridge from the north with a southbound freight. *22 September 1966.*

96 *(left, above)*
90 NY 568128
A very similar working: this time it is Class 5 4–6–0 No 45274, a stablemate from Kingmoor shed, heading south with an up freight. The quarry at Hardendale is located to the right of the sidings in the foreground and roughly in line with the signal box. The locomotive was withdrawn in May 1967 and cut up at McWilliam's, Shettleston, in November that year. *22 September 1966.*

97 *(left, below)*
90 NY 569131
Some nine months later Ivo again visited the location and captured for posterity Stanier 'Black Five' No 44732, in charge of a train of fitted vans, pounding up the 1:106 gradient and heading south towards Shap Summit some two miles distant. The Stanier, from 8A Springs Branch depot (Wigan) had only two weeks or so left in service, being withdrawn at the end of the month; it was scrapped at Cashmore's, Great Bridge, the following March. *16 June 1967.*

98
90 NY 570133
A large quarry situated on the east side of the line, with its attendant sidings, gave Ivo Peters the opportunity to photograph a working known as the 'Hardendale shunt'. Here BR 9F 2–10–0 No 92112, from Birkenhead (8H) shed, stands at the entrance to the quarry sidings with its loaded mineral train, whilst Kingmoor (12A) Britannia Pacific No 70038 (formerly *Robin Hood*) passes by with a southbound freight on the main line. Just visible over the Standard 9F's wagons is the impressive dam of Wet Sleddale reservoir, beyond which are the Shap Fells. Today the quarry is owned by British Steel Strip Products. *22 September 1966.*

Map 4
Shap: Grayrigg and Lowgill (1920)

Thrimby Grange
99
90 NY 557201
Thrimby Bridge, about 2¹/₂ miles north of Shap village and near Thrimby Grange, with the infant River Leith in the foreground and the large oak tree partly shrouding it, proved an ideal setting to capture Stanier Class 5 No 45363 climbing hard on the 1:125 gradient with a southbound empty stone train. Judging by the voluminous black smoke issuing from its chimney, which conveniently hides the pylon in the background, the 'Black Five's fireman is hard at work, helping to make this a dramatic picture. *20 September 1966.*

100 *(left, above)*
90 NY 559200
This photograph, taken from the east side of the line near Thrimby Bridge, shows a weary-looking Royal Scot in its last throes with a northbound ballast train. Class 7P No 46115 *Scots Guardsman* was withdrawn a matter of days after this picture was taken, but survives today, and, at the time of writing, is preserved in 'cosmetic' form at the Birmingham Railway Museum, Tyseley. *22 April 1965.*

101 *(left, below)*
90 NY 558200
With the River Leith nestling close to the line at this point, ex-Crosti BR 9F 2–10–0 No 92024 climbs past Thrimby Grange with an up freight. The locomotive from 8H Birkenhead shed would work for another 2½ years before finally being withdrawn from service. *22 April 1965.*

Plumpton
102
90 NY 496334
Plumpton, some way north of Penrith, was only visited by Ivo on the one occasion when he photographed this 5A Crewe (North) Britannia Pacific, No 70044 *Earl Haig*, in filthy condition and minus its nameplates, passing by at speed with the 10.40am London–Carlisle service. The meandering course of the River Petteril helps to make this an attractive lineside location; this is about a half-mile east of Junction 41 off the M6. *15 April 1965.*

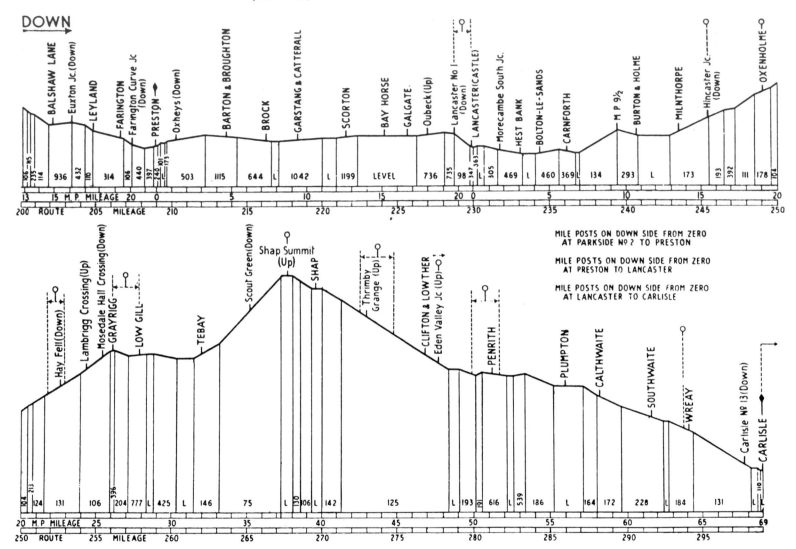

DOWN →

MILE POSTS ON DOWN SIDE FROM ZERO
AT PARKSIDE Nº 2 TO PRESTON

MILE POSTS ON DOWN SIDE FROM ZERO
AT PRESTON TO LANCASTER

MILE POSTS ON DOWN SIDE FROM ZERO
AT LANCASTER TO CARLISLE

Grayrigg

103 *(right)*

97 SD 605962

A very sick diesel: English Electric Type 4 1Co-Co1 No D325 (Class 40 TOPS No 40125), from 5A Crewe (North) depot, in charge of a Birmingham–Glasgow express, has trouble with its 2,000hp EE 16SVT Mk II engine and limps away from Grayrigg firing on about half of the sixteen cylinders. According to Ivo, it sounded like a 'Brock's benefit'—and the smell of its exhaust was awful, truly earning the title 'stinker', which he dubbed all diesel locomotives!

Introduced in November 1960, the locomotive was withdrawn from service in May 1981. Of interest to diesel experts is the split indicator panel fitted to this locomotive. *14 September 1966.*

HAIL TO THE DIESEL!

*A small photographic selection of diesel workings
in Westmorland*

104
97 SD 605962
Dominated by the 2,042ft-high Fell Head, the beautiful Howgill Fells stand out clearly in the background on this lovely summer's day. Resplendent in its two-tone green livery, Crewe-built Brush Type 4 diesel-electric No D1852 (Class 47/0 TOPS No 47202), then just a year old, rounds the bend from Cowperthwaite and approaches Grayrigg with the up 'Royal Scot'. No 47202 was withdrawn from service in March 1987, following a collision in the West Country, and was cut up at Bristol Bath Road Depot during September 1991, being deemed to be beyond economical repair. *14 July 1966.*

Dillicar Common
105
97 SD 623984
A leaden summer sky heavy with rain showers hangs over the Howgills as a Birmingham–Glasgow express headed by Brush Type 4 diesel-electric No D1821 (Class 47/3 TOPS No 47350) speeds round the bend from Lowgill and enters the section leading through the Lune Gorge. The grazing sheep are totally oblivious to the train, remaining undisturbed as they get on with the more important job of extracting nourishment from the rather poor quality grass. Currently painted in the old Railfreight livery, No 47350 is still in use today and based at Tinsley TMD, Sheffield. *12 August 1967.*

The Lune Gorge
106
97 SD 622990
An unidentified two-tone green livery Brush Type 4 diesel-electric roars through the Lune Gorge with an up express. Careful study will reveal two crew members in the cab: a driver and 'fireman'. This was a legacy from steam days, which the unions encouraged, and one of the duties of the second man was to operate the steam heating boiler on some diesel locomotive classes, but this practice has since been discontinued. *14 September 1966.*

Dillicar troughs
107
91 NY 610024
A Glasgow–Birmingham express hauled by English Electric Type 4 1Co-Co1 No D234 (Class 40 TOPS No 40034 *Accra*), then seven years old, passes over Dillicar troughs in the Lune Gorge on a bright but cloudy summer's day. With the advent of the diesel age, the water level in the troughs was lowered in an attempt to reduce oxidisation of the tracks. No 40034, one of the batch fitted with disc-type indicators, was withdrawn in January 1984. *16 July 1966.*

Map 5
Shap: Scout Green and Shap Wells (1920)

Galloway Stone

B.M.898·2

Queens Monument

Old Wells

Rises

909

G.P.

877

B.M.932·5

Quarry

B.M.1194·2

Spring

B.M.904·9

B.M.1116·8

Spa Well (Saline)

F.B.

F.P.

F.P.

B.M.984·2

Quarry

M.S. Orton 2

B.M.1042·2

Tank

Shap Wells Hotel

Old Limekiln

912

F.P.

Quarries

Howe Nook

F.B.

Salterwath Cottages

B.M.1020·5

F.P.

Old Quarries

B.M.968·1

Rises

Sheepfold

Quarry

Thunder Stone

Salterwath

Rises

1008

Quarries

Ford

Quarry

Union & R.D. By.

B.M.910·7

Old Quarry

Old Limekiln

B.M.953·3

Castlehowe Spr.

Springs

Old Quarries

Castle Howe

897

S.P.

W

Haybank

Old Limekiln

900

CROSBY RAVENSWORTH

(Det. No. 6)

889

Bield

964

Rises

Rises

Rises

Docker Force

Rises

Union & R.D. By

Stonygill

F.B.

Rises

B.M.851·3

Sheepfold

Birk Beck

Rises

900

Spring

Rises

Rises

Gibsonhill

F.B.

900

Sheepfolds

B.M.819·7

Spring

852

ORTON
(Det. No. 2)

Green Brow

B.M.750·1

S.P.

Scoutgreen Crossing

1000

East Ward Union
(Det. No. 2)

Undivided Moor

East Westmorland R.D.
(Det. No. 2)

Acres 78·341

Rises

Union & R.D. By.

Rises

Old Limekiln

Rampshowe

B.M.585·7

Union & R.D. By.

M.P.

Shepherd's Bridge

Union & R.D. By

Rises

CROSBY RAVENSWORTH
(Det. No. 6)

Beck

Stakeley Beck

Rises

Ford

F.P.

Scoutgreen

B.M.643·4

W

Sproatg

Union & R.D. By

Shap Wells
108
91 NY 580100
Powering up the final section to Shap Summit with twelve coaches plus a parcels van, which constitutes a London–Glasgow express working, Brush Type 4 Co-Co diesel-electric No D1851 (Class 47/0 TOPS No 47201), shows by the exhaust from its 2,580hp Sulzer engine that it is working hard to lift this heavy train up the 1:75 gradient. Today No 47201 works out of Tinsley TMD, Sheffield, and is in Railfreight Distribution livery. *13 July 1966.*

127

109

91 NY 580100

A much easier task for this English Electric Type 4 1Co-Co1 diesel-electric as it growls its way towards the summit in charge of the eight-coach (FO) Euston–Perth train. Rolling stock experts will notice that the leading Mk1 coach has been fitted with B4 bogies and must have been one of the first of the type to be converted. Ivo identified the locomotive as D326 (Class 40 TOPS No 40126), which was the unfortunate member of the class to be involved in the Great Train Robbery at Sears Crossing, north of Cheddington, LMR, on 8 August 1963. The centre indicator panel would suggest this is actually a candidate which failed the identity parade, as D326 was fitted with the split-type indicator! The locomotive is probably D376, which did have the centre type.

As a point of interest, D326 was introduced in December 1960 and withdrawn in February 1984, after just over 23 years of eventful service and cut up for scrap within two months, thus denying the preservationists any chance of saving this historic locomotive. No D376 (No 40176), introduced in February 1962, only survived until May 1981, when it was withdrawn from service. *11 August 1967.*

Docker Viaduct *(right)*

97 SD 565956

Situated some 10 miles from Milthorpe, the start of the 13-mile climb to Grayrigg, the end of the first of two sections of the ascent to Shap Summit, the six-arch stone viaduct provides an attractive setting to view a 2–6–4T banker as it returns bunker first on the ruling 1:106/131 downgrade to Oxenholme. *30 July 1965.*

THE COLOUR OF
WESTMORLAND STEAM

Photographs by Angela O'Shea

Grayrigg
97 SD 597960
Stanier Class 8F 2–8–0 No 48775, with a permanent way train of new rail sections for continuous welded track, rounds the curve on the approach to Grayrigg. Note the 60mph speed limit sign on the side of the line. On reaching Tebay, the train will require banking assistance from a 2–6–4T up the final section to Shap Summit. *13 April 1966.*

Grayrigg
97 SD 597960
One for the diesel enthusiast: English Electric Type 4 1Co-Co1 (Class 40) No D329 passes the disused station at Grayrigg with an up fitted freight. The breathtaking beauty of Westmorland is self-evident in this view taken on a sunny spring evening, which shows the western slopes of Langdale Fell still adorned with the last traces of snow reluctant to melt away. D329 (TOPS No 40129) was withdrawn from service in May 1984. *13 April 1966.*

Grayrigg
97 SD 603962
Having banked a freight from Oxenholme, Stanier 2–6–4T No 42439 from Tebay shed (12E) enters Grayrigg's down loop to await the passing of an express prior to crossing over to the up line before making its way back downhill for its next turn of duty. The crossover between the up and down lines is in the foreground; and seen in the distance is Grayrigg signal box, which controlled it. *30 July 1965.*

Grayrigg *(right)*
97 SD 604962
Spring view: having a clear road, Class 8F 2–8–0 No 48323 from Rose Grove shed storms past Grayrigg's down loop with a long train of empty wagons. Leaning out from the cab, the 8F's fireman appears to be lost in his thoughts as he takes a breather in preparation for the second phase of the northbound assault to Shap Summit. *14 April 1966.*

Grayrigg
97 SD 604962
Summer view: taken from the same spot a few months earlier, Stanier Class 5 4–6–0 No 45094 in charge of a down parcels train makes a good picture, despite its rather grubby appearance. In the foreground is the bracket signal for Grayrigg's up loop, access to which is just a few yards beyond. *30 July 1965.*

Cowperthwaite
97 SD 610964
This photograph, taken looking due west in the early morning on a lovely summer's day, shows Stanier 'Black Five' No 45449 at the head of a northbound freight as it sweeps through the cutting and under an occupation bridge between Grayrigg and Lowgill. Today a bridge carrying the M6 cuts diagonally across the line replacing the furthest brick and stone overbridge, whilst the one in the foreground has been demolished and supplanted by a concrete structure, which spans not only the railway but also the motorway. *30 July 1965.*

Cowperthwaite
97 SD 610964
A view in the opposite direction shows Stanier Class 5 4–6–0 No 45056 with a southbound special freight, which includes trestle wagons loaded with what appears to be steel plate, rounding the bend from Lowgill. Standing out on this clear spring day, the slopes of the distant Howgills still have traces of snow on the sheltered rock faces and fissures. The M6 now nestles close to the down line behind where the stone wall tops the embankment in this shot. *14 April 1966.*

135

Lowgill
97 SD 621971
BR Caprotti Class 5 4–6–0 No 73140 on an up freight passes Lowgill box and the junction for the disused line that passed through the Lune valley via Sedbergh, Ingleton and to the 'other' Clapham Junction. The line closed in 1964. *14 April 1966.*

Lune's Bridge, Tebay *(right)*
91 NY 614029
Seen from the main A685 road just south of Tebay, which crosses the swiftly-flowing River Lune at this point, is the Kingmoor shedded Stanier 'Black Five' 4–6–0 No 45363 passing over Bridge 106 and running north with a down parcels train. Of interest to the car enthusiast is what looks like a two-tone Ford Zodiac visible on the extreme left with a wooden canoe strapped to its roof. The fell in the background is Jeffery's Mount, the summit of which is some 1,240ft above mean sea level. Today the M6 is sandwiched between it and the railway line. *30 July 1965.*

Dillicar troughs
91 NY 612025
Having a lineside permit has its advantages, but also its drawbacks: the opportunity to record steam locomotives replenishing their water supply as they passed over Dillicar troughs, set between spectacular mountains in the northern end of the Lune Gorge, was a good one, but it also ran the risk of the photographer getting a soaking if standing too close to the line. Fortunately, on this occasion no involuntary shower was taken by Angela O'Shea as she stood on the opposite side of the line to Stanier 'Black Five' No 45094 in charge of a northbound freight, which 'takes a dip'! *14 April 1966.*

138

Greenholme
91 NY 602059
Unsung heroes of the assault of the climb to Shap Summit were the Tebay bankers, which did sterling work and performed several such duties in a day. Seen here in this early morning view is Fairburn 2–6–4T No 42210 pushing hard at the rear of the train, as it assists Stanier Class 5 4–6–0 No 45082 with a northbound freight, which includes several oil tank wagons, and is approaching Greenholme some 1½ miles north of Tebay. A stiff north-easterly wind ensures the locomotives' exhausts are blown across the fields away from the line. *13 April 1966.*

Greenholme
91 NY 602059
Seen on another duty later on the same morning at the same location, Fairburn 2–6–4T No 42210 banks a long northbound freight of mixed wagons, which includes bulk tanks. The train engine on this occasion was 8A Springs Branch (Wigan) 'Black Five' No 45449. Note the up line has recently been replaced with welded rail, whilst those for the down side await positioning, replacing the old. *13 April 1966.*

Greenholme
91 NY 602059
Passing under Scotchman's Bridge, locally known as Scotty's Bridge, which carries a minor road between Orton and Greenholme, Class 9F 2–10–0 No 92076 from Carlisle Kingmoor shed (12A) drifts down from Scout Green with a southbound freight. These powerful locomotives were well able to cope with the arduous climb to Shap, but still required assistance on most northbound freight workings. *13 April 1966.*

Greenholme
91 NY 602061
With few exceptions, the last days of the Kingmoor shedded Britannias were spent on humble freight duties over Shap. Here Britannia class 4–6–2 No 70040 *Clive of India*, minus its nameplates, on a southbound fitted freight, coasts down the 1:75 gradient through the cutting just north of the minor road bridge at Greenholme. *13 April 1966.*

Scout Green
91 NY 597079
This scene is the epitome of Westmorland in steam days: the portrayal of the struggle that locomotives had as they tackled the long northward climb of Shap could not be demonstrated better as in this fine photograph. Taken very early on a cold spring morning, with a strong north-easterly wind blowing, an unidentified Stanier 8F 2–8–0 climbs towards Scout Green with a northbound freight, assisted by a Fairburn 2–6–4T banking hard in the rear. *14 April 1966.*

Scout Green
91 NY 597079
Although caught in the light of the early morning sun, one still cannot identify this Stanier Class 8F, its cabside number partly obscured by grime and typically in a poor state of cleanliness. The 2–8–0, still working hard with some three miles to go before Shap Summit is reached, approaches the diminutive Scout Green box located on the down side of the line one hundred yards or so north of this point. *14 April 1966.*

Shap Wells
91 NY 580100
Nearly there with about a mile to go: viewed from the location Ivo Peters dubbed 'Classic', Stanier 'Black Five' No 45228 assisted by Fairburn 2–6–4T No 42095, one of a batch built in 1949, approaches Shap Wells as it nears the summit of the climb from Tebay, some four miles south. On a clear day the view from this spot was magnificent, but on this occasion the weather was typically dull and overcast with a blustery wind blowing from the north-west. *28 July 1965.*

Sherwood Brow
110 *(right)*
98 SD 814683
An unidentified Stanier Class 5 4–6–0 with a down freight crosses the River Ribble in the Stainforth gorge on this graceful viaduct (No 27), some five miles north of Settle Junction. Ahead of the locomotive lay a further ten miles of the arduous northbound climb at a ruling gradient of 1:100 to Blea Moor on the 'Long Drag', as the steeply-graded Settle & Carlisle line was known. Although a notable shot, this clearly shows the hazards posed by a multitude of telegraph poles and wires when photographing trains in the days before electric signalling! *9 August 1967.*

Thrimby Grange
90 NY 557201
Making plenty of smoke which conveniently blots out the electricity pylons in the background, Stanier Class 5 4–6–0 No 45039 charges up the 1:125 ruling gradient and under the minor road bridge near Thrimby Grange as it heads towards Shap with a southbound freight. The northern approach to Shap Summit from Penrith was somewhat easier with no section graded steeper than 1:106. Despite the pylons, this was a popular spot to watch trains: the elegant stone bridge (No 142) and river in the foreground helping to make the setting attractive. *13 April 1966.*

AU REVOIR, SETTLE & CARLISLE STEAM

*The last fifteen months of regular BR steam operation
over the 'Long Drag'*

Helwith Bridge
111
98 SD 810697
Helwith Bridge, some four miles from Settle, only provided a short respite for northbound locomotives on a level stretch for less than a half-mile, before the line climbed again at 1:100. Crossing the River Ribble on this most attractive bridge is Stanier Class 8F 2–8–0 No 48773, then from 9K Bolton depot, with a down freight.

It befell No 48773 to be the last locomotive in steam at the Rose Grove shed (10F), where it spent its final days in BR service. Its last duty was to work a LCGB 'farewell' special from Blackburn to Carnforth on 4 August 1968, then it was withdrawn. After a varied and chequered history, the locomotive escaped the cutter's torch and has been preserved: it is usually based on the Severn Valley Railway, Bridgnorth, Shropshire, but now sports a 66A Polmadie (Glasgow) shed code; the last time it carried this was in 1962. *10 August 1967.*

112
98 SD 810696
On this rather dull day with poor visibility, a thoroughly grimy BR Class 9F 2–10–0, unidentifiable with its smokebox and cabside number obliterated by layers of grime, gathers speed on the short level stretch as it passes Helwith Bridge with a Bescot-Carlisle freight. *10 August 1967.*

Batty Moss Viaduct, Ribblehead
114
98 SD 760788

Even though it was a hazy day, there can be few photographs taken in steam days to match this shot of a Standard Class 9F 2–10–0 in charge of an up freight crossing the magnificent 24-arch Batty Moss Viaduct at Ribblehead. There has been much written about this structure, which is synonymous with the S&C—and is its Achilles' heel. The line's future may well depend on it, as in the past when extensive and costly repairs threatened its existence in the 1980s.

Set in splendid isolation surrounded by moorland—save for a few cottages and a pub—the atrocious weather conditions, particularly the legendary high winds experienced here, often made it a bleak and inhospitable place to be. But on this warm and sunny September day, with the outline of Winterscales Pasture on Whernside visible in the distance, it must have been an idyllic spot for Ivo to while away an hour or two photographing trains accompanied by the 'vee-veet' call of a lapwing or melodious song of a lark drifting down from somewhere high in the heavens, perhaps disturbed only by the infrequent passing of a car on the nearby B6255 road. *23 September 1966.*

113
98 SD 810696

A sequential shot shows the 9F leaving a trail of thick black smoke in its wake, about to tackle the unrelenting nine-mile climb to Blea Moor Tunnel, before the summit is reached at Ais Gill, a further nine miles beyond. The Ribble holds some interest to the footplate crew, who look down into the clear water, perhaps gauging the size of any trout that might be lurking in the lee of the bridge!

By way of contrast to the clarity of the river, the hazy conditions all but obscure the distinctive craggy outline of the 2,277ft peak of Pen-y-Gent, the slopes of which can just be made out on the right of the picture. *10 August 1967.*

115

98 SD 760788

A photograph such as this could not show more clearly the remoteness and
rugged splendour of the countryside traversed by the railway as illustrated in this
view taken at Ribblehead of a BR Standard Class 4 2–6–0 in charge of a three-
coach down local, apparently with not a soul on board, as it approaches the
viaduct on the embankment set between it and the station, which, along with
Dent and Horton-in-Ribblesdale, officially closed to passengers on 4 May 1970.
When the line was threatened with closure in the 1980s, the stationmasters'
houses were sold by British Rail and became private dwellings. However,
following the line's reprieve in recent years, with support from the Yorkshire
Dales National Park and tourist authorities, all scheduled trains (currently Class
156 'SuperSprinter' units) still stop there today; but in the case of Ribblehead
station, it is in the southbound direction only, since there is no platform left on
the down side. The remaining station buildings there are now derelict.
23 September 1967.

116

98 SD 758795

An unidentified Stanier Class 5, with a northbound freight, seems almost dwarfed
in this worm's eye view of Batty Moss Viaduct, the highest arch of which is some
165ft above ground level. The ¼-mile long viaduct took nearly five years to build
at great cost to the Midland Railway. The structure's first opportunity to bear the
weight of a revenue-earning train was on 1 November 1875, when the line
opened for goods traffic, but passengers were not able to cross it until 1 May
1876. *21 April 1967.*

117
98 SD 757796
Taken from the north-western end of the viaduct, this superb study shows Britannia class No 70010 *Owen Glendower* crossing with a short northbound freight. Although the viaduct is still in use today, albeit with the line reduced to a single track and trains restricted to 30mph, No 70010 did not survive and was withdrawn from traffic in September 1967, just five months after this photograph was taken. *21 April 1967.*

Blea Moor
118
98 SD 757800

This is one of the very few photographs taken by Ivo on the Settle & Carlisle line previously published and shows the omnipresent Kingmoor shed Class 9F 2–10–0 No 92019 leaving the wilds of Blea Moor as it sets off south with the up 'Long Meg' freight of anhydrite to Widnes. The 9F was nearing the end of its working life and was withdrawn just over a month after this photograph was taken. In the background are the signals set at the southern end of the Blea Moor loops, half-way along which is the box that controls them.

Following the line being singled across the Ribblehead viaduct and for a few chains north, the down loop has lost its southern connection to the main line and remains as a long siding accessible only by a trailing point at the northern end. *21 April 1967.*

Blea Moor Tunnel
119
98 SD 777840
Seen leaving the north portal of the 2,629yd Blea Moor Tunnel is Class 9F 2–10–0 No 92012 with a down freight. Having left behind the worst of the 15-mile climb from Settle Junction, fittingly dubbed the 'Long Drag', ahead lay a fairly easy stretch at moderate grades to the summit at Ais Gill, from where the line would descend towards Carlisle. No 92012 from Carlisle Kingmoor MPD had only two months of service left, for it was withdrawn in October the same year. *8 August 1967.*

Dent Head
120
98 SD 778841
On a hazy September afternoon Class 5 4–6–0, thought to be No 44836 of 9B Stockport shed, sweeps over the ten spans of Dent Head Viaduct with an up banana train. In the background is the disused Dent Head signal box, a lonely outpost set between Blea Moor Tunnel and Dent station. The more observant will notice the signal posts have already lost their arms, which were removed soon after the box was closed; also of note is the double snow fencing on Wold Fell beyond. The viaduct was built in locally quarried limestone and blends in well with stone walling and outbarns, which are very much part of the landscape in the Yorkshire Dales. *23 September 1966.*

121
98 SD 777841
Kingmoor MPD Stanier Class 5 No 44675, heading towards Blea Moor Tunnel with an up freight, is seen passing over the 197ft-long Dent Head Viaduct and the small bridge spanning the minor road from Newby Head, which now forms part of the Dales Way. Rising to 2,205ft in the background is great Knoutberry Hill on Widdale Fell, below which is Dent Fell and Arten Gill. Beyond the cutting in the middle distance is the equally impressive Arten Gill Viaduct. Withdrawn in December that year, No 44675 was cut up by the Motherwell & Machinery Scrap Co Wishaw, in February 1968. *29 April 1967.*

122
98 SD 778846
After emerging from Blea Moor Tunnel in the background, still with smoke drifting from its north portal, a Britannia class Pacific, in frightful external condition making identification impossible, comes charging round the bend with a down freight on the slightly undulating gradient towards the site of Dent Head signal box, which had closed in 1965. The viaduct is a few hundred yards back beyond the crossover. Today much of the northern face of Blea Moor seen in the background over the tunnel has been heavily planted with conifer trees. *18 April 1967.*

Arten Gill Viaduct
123
98 SD 778857
Scenery such as is pictured here and elegant structures like the 11-arch Arten Gill Viaduct, which when combined with a steam locomotive crossing it, provide the perfect recipe for the lineside photographer to capture a memorable study. Here BR Class 9F 2–10–0 No 92051 brings a short southbound freight over the viaduct, which strides across Artengill Beck. The light coloured gable end of the building just visible in the middle distance over the locomotive is Dent station, which at 1,150ft is the highest on a main line in England, is some 450ft above and four miles from the village it purports to serve. Seen in the far distance beyond the station is East Baugh Fell, the highest point of which is Knoutberry Haw at 2,218ft above sea level and stands nearly twice as high. *8 August 1967.*

Garsdale
124
98 SD 788918
Having just crossed Dandrymire Viaduct in the background, Britannia Pacific No 70046 (formerly *Anzac*), in charge of an up freight and in a very sorry state, approaches Garsdale station. The Britannia, then of 12A Kingmoor depot, was withdrawn from service less than three months later, being cut up at Campbell's, Airdrie, in January 1968.

The station, also once known as Hawes Junction, was the point where the Midland constructed a branch from the main line to Hawes, where it joined with the NE branch from Northallerton. The Garsdale to Hawes section, once the province of the famous 'Boniface' Hawes–Bradford Forster Square service, closed to passengers on 16 March 1959, whilst the ex-NE line from Northallerton closed to Hawes on 26 April 1954, but survives as far as Redmire for mineral traffic. The former junction and sidings, the latter of which survive today, are obscured behind the Britannia. *20 April 1967.*

Shotlock Hill Tunnel
125
98 SD 788943
Standard Class 9F No 92125, minus its shed plate but then from Kingmoor depot, bursts out of the southern portal of the 106yd Shotlock Hill Tunnel with a 'Long Meg' freight working and finds the going easy on the falling 1:100 gradient. The tunnel is one of fourteen between Settle and Carlisle and runs very close to the B6259, some 1½ miles north of Garsdale and just a mile or so from both Moorcock Tunnel and the famous Moorcock Inn, which is the only pub for miles around.

The 9F was withdrawn the following December when its depot closed at the end of the year. The locomotive survived only a further four months, before being scrapped in April 1968 by Arnott Young, Parkgate & Rawmarsh. *21 April 1967.*

Ais Gill summit
126
98 SD 780961
The Long Meg sidings to Widnes anhydrite freight workings were once a feature of the S&C line in the latter years of steam. On a misty day which obscures the distant views, Kingmoor Standard Class 9F 2–10–0 No 92015, having just breasted Ais Gill summit with steam to spare, gathers speed on the falling 1:330 gradient with a southbound 'Long Meg'. The 'Long Drag' was over once this point had been reached and firemen could expect a much easier workload from here on. The bridge in the background represents the county border between Westmorland (now Cumbria) and North Yorkshire.

Following closure, the signal box was dismantled and relocated at the Midland Railway Centre, Butterley, where it has been restored. The loops have since been removed. *23 September 1966.*

127
98 SD 780961
Newton Heath (9D) Class 5 4–6–0 No 45101 heads away from Ais Gill with an up freight. With the 1,169ft summit just passed, only a few stretches of rising grades to Blea Moor still have to be tackled; the worst of the southbound climb is over and the crew can look forward to an easy run towards Settle Junction. *18 April 1967.*

128
98 SD 779962
Standing near the signal box, Ivo has a good view on this lovely summer's day of the distinctive outline of Wild Boar Fell, which, rising to 2,323ft, provides an ideal backcloth to photograph another 'Long Meg' anhydrite working. This time it is Carlisle Kingmoor 9F No 92110 in charge which is captured for posterity; it was withdrawn six months later and was scrapped by Arnott Young, Parkgate & Rawmarsh, in March 1968. *12 June 1967.*

129
98 SD 775967
With the slopes of Wild Boar Fell just visible through the haze in the background, BR Class 4 4–6–0 No 75011 climbs towards Ais Gill summit with a southbound mineral train. The 4–6–0 had only a matter of days left in service and was withdrawn at the end of the month. It met its end at Ward's, Beighton, in February 1967. *23 September 1966.*

130
98 SD 775967
This clear spring day provided good views along Mallerstang of trains approaching Ais Gill summit. The bridge in the background, featured in many S&C shots and also a favourite vantage point of photographers, carries the B6259 road.

Here a very grubby Class 8F 2–8–0, No 48421, from 8L Aintree depot, is seen with an empty ICI bulk soda ash train as it tackles the final half-mile stretch of line to the summit. The Stanier was transferred to 8E Northwich shed a month later, from where it was eventually withdrawn in February 1968, before being scrapped at Cashmore's, Newport, in July that year. *29 April 1967.*

Mallerstang
131
98 SD 772984

The now-preserved ex-LMS Jubilee class 4–6–0 No 45593 *Kolhapur*, climbing steadily along Mallerstang Common with a southbound empty freight, crosses the small viaduct spanning Ais Gill, which flows into the River Eden below. The passage of the line cut along the fellside was a remarkable feat of engineering and affords splendid views across to Mallerstang Edge, the pinnacle of which is High Seat at 2,326ft, which can be seen in this view on the right of the picture.

The Leeds Holbeck (55A) Jubilee was not just restricted to freight workings, but also was rostered for the occasional passenger duty until withdrawal from BR service in October 1967. Today it is normally based at the Tyseley depot of the Birmingham Railway Museum, but at the time of writing resides on the Great Central Railway at Loughborough. *18 April 1967.*

Kirkby Stephen West
132
91 NY 763064

Kirkby Stephen once had two stations: this one, about 1½ miles south-west of the village on the Midland's route, and Kirkby Stephen East station, which was nearer the centre of population it served and located near the junction where the ex-NER link from Tebay to Durham (also to Darlington via Barnard Castle) joined with the route from Eden Valley Junction near Penrith, also on the West Coast main line. The well appointed Kirkby Stephen East station, which also had extensive sidings and an engine shed, closed on 20 January 1962. Kirkby Stephen West station on the Midland's S&C line was also adequately equipped and provided with a goods shed, cattle dock, a coal yard as well as up and down loops. The signal box seen here was demolished and rebuilt in 1974, following the discovery that water had ingressed its foundations.

Here Class 9F 2–10–0 No 92071 passes the station and judging by its exhaust is working hard on the rising 1:100 gradient in charge of a southbound special freight of steel ingots carried on bogie bolsters. *23 September 1966.*

167

133
91 NY 763064
Looking in the opposite direction from on top of the embankment, Ivo Peters had this marvellous view on a clear day to Mallerstang Edge in the distance over the other side of the valley. Drifting past the loops is Britannia No 70021 *Morning Star*, in fair condition but deprived of its nameplates, having an easy task with this short northbound freight. The Pacific, then from 9B Stockport MPD, was withdrawn from service at Kingmoor during the following December and was subsequently scrapped at Ward's, Inverkeithing, between March and May the following year. *20 April 1967.*

134
91 NY 763064
Ivo did not have such a clear day a few months before when he photographed Class 8F 2–8–0 No 48708 as it passed the same spot, but in charge of a much longer mixed freight working. The Stanier, then based at 9J Agecroft depot, had some seven months' life left before being withdrawn; it was scrapped at Draper's, Hull, in September 1967. *23 September 1966.*

135

91 NY 763064

Showing little effort as it passes Kirkby Stephen West, is Carlisle Kingmoor Standard Class 9F 2–10–0 No 92056 working an up 'Long Meg' to Widnes. The 9F's fireman jauntily wearing his grease-top cap makes sure he gets in the picture, but unseen is a celebrated passenger on the footplate in the form of Derek Cross, the well-known railway photographer and a friend of Ivo. It was Derek Cross who persuaded Ivo, and was therefore indirectly responsible, to make these trips to the North-West, enabling him to record the last days of steam in the region, which many can share in the form of the photographs he took. *15 June 1967.*

136

91 NY 763064

Stockport (9B) Stanier Class 5 No 45261, then with just four months of working life left, makes a stirring sight in charge of an up freight of empty hoppers as it climbs hard on the rising gradient past Kirkby Stephen's sidings. Although it was closed to passengers from 4 May 1970, the unmanned station is still used today and well patronised, especially in the summer season. In winter six trains a day stop in either direction, but this is increased to eight for the summer timetable. *5 June 1967.*

137
91 NY 764064
Seen passing the old signal box at Kirkby Stephen West with a heavy Carlisle–Crewe freight is Stanier 'Black Five' 4–6–0 No 44859 from 5D Stoke shed and which was withdrawn in November the same year. The tall inner down home signal looks well braced to cope with the strong winds often experienced here, but on this day with only a slight breeze, it was perfectly safe from the elements! Of note is Ivo Peters' Bentley, which he has parked near the signal box ready to make a quick getaway and to take him in a reasonable degree of comfort to the next lineside location. *15 June 1967.*

138
91 NY 763065
Another pleasing trackside shot: this time it is looking in the opposite direction from the other side of the line and depicts 12A Kingmoor shed Class 9F No 92071 returning 'Long Meg' empties from Widnes. Seen just over the train is the roof of the goods shed, which closed for business on 28 September 1964 along with the other facilities. The 9F was cut up by the Motherwell Machinery & Scrap Co Wishaw, in February 1968, having been withdrawn seven months after this photograph was taken.

Today steam is still very much part of the Settle & Carlisle line, for many specials are run over it, which usually are sold out well in advance. Always a magnet for the enthusiast and lineside photographer, their continued appearance on this magnificent route, so much a part of our illustrious railway heritage, will help to earn much-needed revenue ensuring its survival, which is by no means certain in this profit-motivated age. *20 April 1967.*

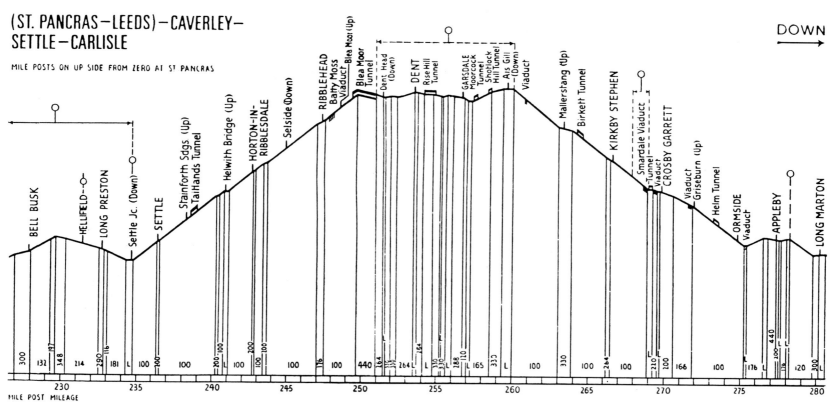

(ST. PANCRAS—LEEDS)—CAVERLEY—
SETTLE—CARLISLE

MILE POSTS ON UP SIDE FROM ZERO AT ST PANCRAS

DOWN →

BELL BUSK

HELLIFIELD

LONG PRESTON

Settle Jc. (Down)

SETTLE

Stainforth Sdgs (Up)
Taithands Tunnel

Helwith Bridge (Up)

HORTON-IN-
RIBBLESDALE

Selside (Down)

RIBBLEHEAD

Batty Moss
Viaduct

Blea Moor (Up)

Blea Moor
Tunnel

Dent Head (Down)

DENT

Rise Hill
Tunnel

GARSDALE
Moorcock
Tunnel

Shotlock
Hill Tunnel

Ais Gill
(Down)

Viaduct

Mallerstang (Up)

Birkett Tunnel

KIRKBY STEPHEN

Smardale Viaduct
Tunnel
Viaduct

CROSBY GARRETT

Viaduct
Griseburn (Up)

Helm Tunnel

ORMSIDE
Viaduct

APPLEBY

LONG MARTON

300 132 348 214 290 181 L 100 100 100 200 100 100 100 100 100 176 100 440 164 135 264 L 154 330 230 288 110 L 165 333 L 100 330 100 264 100 210 100 166 100 176 L 440 200 170 120 300 L

MILE POST MILEAGE

230 235 240 245 250 255 260 265 270 275 280

Withdrawal dates and fate

GWR Class 47XX 2-8-0

CLASS/NUMBER/NAME	SHED*	WITHDRAWN	SCRAPPED/PRESERVED	DATE
4708	81A	10/62	J Cashmore, Great Bridge	8/63–12/63

GWR King class 4-6-0

CLASS/NUMBER/NAME	SHED*	WITHDRAWN	SCRAPPED/PRESERVED	DATE
6009 *King Charles II*	81A	9/62	J Cashmore, Newport	12/62

Fairburn Class 4MT 2-6-4T

CLASS/NUMBER/NAME	SHED*	WITHDRAWN	SCRAPPED/PRESERVED	DATE
42095	12E	6/66	J Cashmore, Great Bridge	8/66
42110	12E	6/66	A Draper, Hull	10/66
42154	10A	1/67	GH Campbell, Airdrie	6/67
42210	12E	5/67	J McWilliam, Shettleston	12/67
42251	12E	10/67	A Draper, Hull	4/68

Stanier Class 4MT 2-6-4T

CLASS/NUMBER/NAME	SHED*	WITHDRAWN	SCRAPPED/PRESERVED	DATE
42439	12E	8/65	Arnott Young, Troon Harbour	9/65–6/68
42665	12E	6/67	A Draper, Hull	1/68

Ivatt Class 4MT 2-6-0

CLASS/NUMBER/NAME	SHED*	WITHDRAWN	SCRAPPED/PRESERVED	DATE
43017	12D	11/67	Motherwell Machinery & Scrap Co Ltd, Wishaw	2/68
43029	12D	9/67	Motherwell Machinery & Scrap Co Ltd, Wishaw	2/68

Stanier Class 5MT 4-6-0

CLASS/NUMBER/NAME	SHED*	WITHDRAWN	SCRAPPED/PRESERVED	DATE
44672	12A	3/68	A Draper, Hull	6/68
44675	12A	9/67	Motherwell Machinery & Scrap Co Ltd, Wishaw	2/68
44677	12A	10/67	J McWilliam, Shettleston	4/68
44732	8F	7/67	J Cashmore, Great Bridge	1/68
44758	10J	7/68	G Cohen, Cargo Fleet, Middlesbrough	10/68–12/68
44767 *George Stephenson#*	12A	12/67	**Preserved: North Yorkshire Moors Railway, Grosmont**	
44795	12A	7/67	J McWilliam, Shettleston	12/67
44832	5B	9/67	Thomas Ward, Killamarsh, Sheffield	12/67
44836	9B	5/68	Thomas Ward, Beighton, Sheffield	9/68
44858	12A	12/67	Thomas Ward, Beighton, Sheffield	3/68
44859	5D	11/67	J Cashmore, Great Bridge	3/68
44886	12A	10/67	Motherwell Machinery & Scrap Co Ltd, Wishaw	3/68
44900	12A	6/67	J McWilliam, Shettleston	11/67
44915	10D	12/67	Thomas Ward, Beighton, Sheffield	10/68
44917	6B	11/67	J Cashmore, Great Bridge	3/68
44937	12A	5/67	J McWilliam, Shettleston	11/67
44964	8A	10/67	J Cashmore, Great Bridge	3/68
44986	12A	5/67	J McWilliam, Shettleston	11/67
45005	8A	1/68	G Cohen, Kettering	8/68
45039	8A	8/67	J Buttigieg, Newport	3/68
45048	8F	11/67	A Draper, Hull	2/68
45056	5B	8/67	J Buttigieg, Newport	12/67–3/68
45069	8A	6/67	G Cohen, Kettering	12/67
45082	12A	7/66	Motherwell Machinery & Scrap Co Ltd, Wishaw	10/66
45093	5B	11/65	J Cashmore, Great Bridge	12/65–2/66
45094	8A	2/67	A Draper, Hull	9/67
45101	9D	3/68	A Draper, Hull	7/68
45105	12A	10/66	J McWilliam, Shettleston	2/67
45109	8B	4/67	G Cohen, Kettering	9/67
45118	12A	10/66	A Draper, Hull	3/67
45120	12A	6/67	Motherwell Machinery & Scrap Co Ltd, Wishaw	11/67
45126	12A	5/67	J McWilliam, Shettleston	11/67
45135	12A	10/67	J McWilliam, Shettleston	3/68
45187	8A	6/68	A Draper, Hull	10/68–3/69
45198	8F	9/67	J Cashmore, Great Bridge	7/68
45209	10A	6/68	A Draper, Hull	10/68
45210	12A	4/66	Motherwell Machinery & Scrap Co Ltd, Wishaw	7/66
45228	12A	3/67	GH Campbell, Airdrie	12/67
45232	8H	11/67	J Cashmore, Great Bridge	3/68
45236	12A	12/67	Thomas Ward, Inverkeithing	4/68
45259	12A	12/67	Thomas Ward, Beighton, Sheffield	4/68
45261	9B	10/67	J Cashmore, Newport	2/68
45274	12A	5/67	J McWilliam, Shettleston	11/67
45295	12A	12/67	Thomas Ward, Beighton, Sheffield	4/68
45310	8F	8/68	G Cohen, Cargo Fleet, Middlesbrough	12/68
45330	8L	8/68	J Cashmore, Newport	12/68
45353	10D	7/68	G Cohen, Kettering	2/69
45363	12A	10/67	J McWilliam, Shettleston	3/68
45395	8F	3/68	J Cashmore, Newport	7/68
45421	10C	2/68	Thomas Ward, Beighton, Sheffield	6/68
45431	8F	11/67	A Draper, Hull	5/68
45445	10A	6/68	A Draper, Hull	10/68
45449	8F	11/67	A Draper, Hull	2/68
45450	10D	11/67	J Cashmore, Great Bridge	2/68
45455	12A	8/67	J McWilliam, Shettleston	2/68

Patriot Class 6P 4-6-0

CLASS/NUMBER/NAME	SHED*	WITHDRAWN	SCRAPPED/PRESERVED	DATE
45531 *Sir Frederick Harrison*	12A	11/65	GH Campbell, Airdrie	1/66–3/66

Jubilee Class 6P 4-6-0

CLASS/NUMBER/NAME	SHED*	WITHDRAWN	SCRAPPED/PRESERVED	DATE
45593 *Kolhapur*	55A	10/67	**Preserved: Birmingham Railway Museum, Tyseley**	
45627 *Sierra Leone*	8K	9/66	J Cashmore, Great Bridge	2/67
45698 *Mars*	8K	11/65	Thomas Ward, Beighton, Sheffield	2/66

Royal Scot Class 7P 4–6–0

46115 Scots Guardsman	12A	12/65
46160 Queen Victoria's Rifleman	12A	5/65

Stanier Class 8F 2–8–0

48211	10D	11/67	J Buttigieg, Newport	3/68
48214	9H	11/67	A Draper, Hull	3/68
48323	10F	6/68	A Draper, Hull	12/68
48421	8L	2/68	J Cashmore, Newport	7/68
48528	8A	8/67	J Buttigieg, Newport	12/67
48708	9J	4/67	A Draper, Hull	9/67
48723	6A	8/68	Thomas Ward, Beighton, Sheffield	12/68
48773	9K	8/68		
48775	9D	8/68		

BR Standard Britannia Class 7P 4–6–2

70005 John Milton	12A	7/67	GH Campbell, Airdrie	1/68
70006 Robert Burns	12A	5/67	J McWilliam, Shettleston	11/67
70010 Owen Glendower	12A	9/67	J McWilliam, Shettleston	1/68
70011 Hotspur	12A	12/67	J McWilliam, Shettleston	4/68
70013 Oliver Cromwell	12A	8/68		
70018 Flying Dutchman	12B	12/66		
70021 Morning Star	9B	12/67	Thomas Ward, Inverkeithing	3/68–5/68
70022 Tornado	12A	12/67	Thomas Ward, Inverkeithing	4/68
70023 Venus	5B	12/67	Thomas Ward, Killamarsh, Sheffield	4/68
70024 Vulcan	12A	12/67	Thomas Ward, Killamarsh, Sheffield	4/68
70025 Western Star	5B/12A	12/67	GH Campbell, Airdrie	1/68
70027 Rising Star	5B	6/67		
70028 Royal Star	5B/12A	12/67	GH Campbell, Airdrie	1/68
70031 Byron	12A	11/67	J McWilliam, Shettleston	3/68
70032 Tennyson	12A/12B	9/67	J McWilliam, Shettleston	3/68
70033 Charles Dickens	12A	7/67	GH Campbell, Airdrie	6/68
70034 Thomas Hardy	5A	5/67	J McWilliam, Shettleston	10/67
70038 Robin Hood	12A	8/67	J McWilliam, Shettleston	2/68
70039 Sir Christopher Wren	12A	9/67	J McWilliam, Shettleston	2/68
70040 Clive of India	12A	4/67	J McWilliam, Shettleston	12/67
70044 Earl Haig	5A	1/67	Thomas Ward, Beighton, Sheffield	2/67
70046 Anzac	12A	7/67	GH Campbell, Airdrie	1/68
70048 The Territorial Army 1908–1958	12B	5/67	J McWilliam, Shettleston	10/67
70049 Solway Firth	12B	12/67	J McWilliam, Shettleston	3/68
70050 Firth of Clyde	5A	8/66	GH Campbell, Airdrie	12/66

BR Standard Class 5MT 4–6–0

73140	9H	10/67	J Cashmore, Newport	2/68

BR Standard Class 4MT 4–6–0

75011	10G	10/66	Thomas Ward, Beighton, Sheffield	2/67
75037	12E	12/67	Arnott Young, Carmyle	7/68

Preserved: Birmingham Railway Museum, Tyseley
Motherwell Machinery & Scrap Co Ltd, Wishaw 7/65

Preserved: Severn Valley Railway, Bridgnorth, Shropshire
Thomas Ward, Beighton, Sheffield 12/68

Preserved: Bressingham Gardens, Diss, Norfolk

BR Standard Class 9F 2–10–0

92009	12A	3/68	J Cashmore, Newport	7/68
92012	12A	10/67	J McWilliam, Shettleston	2/68
92015	12A	5/67	J McWilliam, Shettleston	11/67
92019	12A	6/67	Motherwell Machinery & Scrap Co Ltd, Wishaw	1/68
92021	8H	11/67	GH Campbell, Airdrie	1/68
92024	8H	11/67	GH Campbell, Airdrie	5/68
92051	12A	10/67	Motherwell Machinery & Scrap Co Ltd, Wishaw	2/68
92056	12A	11/67	Motherwell Machinery & Scrap Co Ltd, Wishaw	2/68
92071	12A	11/67	Motherwell Machinery & Scrap Co Ltd, Wishaw	2/68
92076	12A	2/67	J McWilliam, Shettleston	6/67
92093	12A	8/67	Motherwell Machinery & Scrap Co Ltd, Wishaw	2/68
92096	12A	2/67	J McWilliam, Shettleston	6/67
92110	12A	12/67	Arnott Young, Parkgate & Rawmarsh	3/68
92112	8H	11/67	GH Campbell, Airdrie	3/68
92125	12A	12/67	Arnott Young, Parkgate & Rawmarsh	4/68
92160	8B	7/68	GH Campbell, Airdrie	10/68
92233	12A	2/68	Thomas Ward, Beighton, Sheffield	8/68
92249	12A	5/68	Arnott Young, Parkgate & Rawmarsh	9/68

* Allocated shed when photographed   # Named in private ownership

MOTIVE POWER DEPOTS

Codes and closure dates

CODE	LOCATION	CLOSED/ TO STEAM*	CODE	LOCATION	CLOSED/ TO STEAM*
5A	Crewe (North)	–/6/65	9K	Bolton	1/7/68
5B	Crewe (South)	6/11/67	9J	Agecroft	17/10/66
5D	Stoke	6/8/67	10A	Carnforth	5/8/68
6A	Chester	–/6/67*	10C	Fleetwood	14/2/66
6B	Mold Junction	18/4/66	10D	Lostock Hall	5/8/68*
8A	Edge Hill	6/5/68	10F	Rose Grove	5/8/68
8B	Warrington	1/10/67	10G	Skipton	3/4/67
8F	Springs Branch	4/12/67*	10J	Lancaster	18/4/66
8H	Birkenhead	6/11/67*	12A	Carlisle Kingmoor	1/1/68
8K	Bank Hall	17/10/66	12B	Carlisle Upperby	12/12/66
8L	Aintree	12/6/67	12D	Workington	1/1/68
9B	Stockport Edgeley	6/5/68	12E	Tebay	1/1/68
9D	Newton Heath	1/7/68*	55A	Leeds Holbeck	1/10/67*
9H	Patricroft	1/7/68	81A	Old Oak Common	22/3/65*

ACKNOWLEDGEMENTS

The late Ivo Peters wished to express his sincere thanks to Derek Mercer for the excellent printing of his negatives and to Caroline Ingle for typing his original manuscript. He also wished to acknowledge with immense gratitude the help he always received from Angela O'Shea with the books and articles he wrote over the years.

As the writer, I would also like to express my thanks to the following for the help received in the preparation of this volume. Firstly to Julian Peters, without whose permission this project would not have left the stocks, but especially for his help in selecting additional negatives from his father's collection for printing and inclusion in the book; secondly, both to Murray Brown of *Rail* magazine and to Peter Hands of Defiant Publications, who supplied much of the historical information and the fate of individual locomotives featured in this work. Finally, to Lydia Peters and to my wife Jenny for the tolerance they have shown in reading through the manuscript.

Mac Hawkins   1992